ADOPTED FOR DAILY LIFE
a devotional for adopting moms

ABOUT THE AUTHOR/EDITOR

Wendy Willard is an author, designer, and adoption care worker. She and her husband founded FIT (Families in Transition) in Nicaragua to meet the physical, emotional, and spiritual needs of families traveling to adopt there. Over the last decade, she and her husband have fostered at least 17 kids, between the ages of 15 months and 17 years, in the U.S., and cared for more than 25 adopting families in Nicaragua. She is also the mom to two teenage girls. Wendy blogs about her adventures at **STILLNOTTHEREYET.COM**.

ADOPTED FOR DAILY LIFE
a devotional for adopting moms

Wendy Willard

Author/Editor	Wendy Willard
Copy Editor	Alisha Forrest
Layout/Design	Wendy Willard
Cover Photo	jumaydesigns via istockphoto.com

v.04252015

introduction

The first six months of any adoption are the most critical as families transition to a new normal. Fear, worry, and disappointment are all common during that time. But—if we remain focused on God's purpose and promise—hope, faith, comfort, and peace can be just as common.

This devotional offers weekly readings for that pivotal season of bonding and transition, as well as for other times when adopting moms need encouragement and refreshment. Each week, *moms who've been there* offer insight on life topics as they relate to adoption. The daily selections are rooted in scripture, to ensure you stay grounded safely in God's Word throughout the journey. Any weeks that do not otherwise list an author were written by me.

TOPICS COVERED

» *adoption*, page 8

» *self-care*, page 15

» *faith*, page 21

» *barrenness*, page 27

» *worry*, page 34

» *beholding Christ*, page 40

» *fear*, page 48

» *trust*, page 54

» *joy*, page 60

» *disappointment*, page 66

» *hope*, page 72

» *depression*, page 78

» *failure*, page 85

» *humility*, page 92

» *anger*, page 98

» *spiritual warfare*, page 105

» *purpose*, page 112

» *waiting*, page 118

» *endurance*, page 124

» *loss*, page 130

» *providence*, page 136

» *his presence*, page 143

» *his faithfulness*, page 150

» *my shepherd*, page 157

» *remembering*, page 164

» *peace*, page 170

» *love*, page 176

Note: *The order in which the themes appear in this book is merely one possible way in which they may be read. If the week focused on humility really speaks to you, perhaps you will return to it several times before continuing. Or if you are experiencing a distinct period of anxiety, consider reading all of the fear, worry, and peace weeks in succession. Starting to really question God's plan? Check out the weeks starting with anger, spiritual warfare, and purpose. We hope you find this book to be a reference for what God has to say about each of the topics, specifically as they relate to adoption. Indexes of* **CONTRIBUTORS** *and* **SCRIPTURE** *are available at the end of the book.*

HOW THIS BOOK CAME TO BE

God gave me the idea for this book as I began an adoption care ministry in Nicaragua. But, like many suggestions God makes, I ignored it for a few months (OK, maybe a year or so). Until eventually, he brought it up again while I was driving through cornfields in eastern Indiana. As I tried once more to ignore the idea, a radio ad woke me from those thoughts of avoidance. "Is there a book God has been asking you to write?" the announcer started out. "OK, already!" I responded.

Within a few days, almost two-dozen adoptive moms spread across the globe agreed to join me and the *Adopted for Daily Life* devotional was born.

HOW THIS BOOK IS UNIQUE

This book is written by adoptive moms for adoptive moms, so together we can brave the season of transition to stay focused on Christ. It is a labor of love created by a group of volunteers who love Jesus and love to see the fatherless become orphans-no-more.

This book is not a self-help book; it is a devotional for Christ-followers. Instead of telling adoption stories and merely adding in some glib scripture references, the writers crafted each devotion around specific scripture that spoke to them during their adoption—words God used to remind them of his purpose and promise at a time when they desperately needed it. Some weeks feature a single scriptural focus (highlighted at the start of the week), while others use several verses from different books of the Bible, weaved throughout the readings, to support the topic.

The moms who contributed represent families grown through both domestic and foreign adoptions from all over the world, including China, Guatemala, Nicaragua, Poland, Korea, and Ethiopia.

All proceeds from this book support adoptions and adoption care through the FIT (Families in Transition) ministry in Nicaragua as well as its global expansion efforts. Visit **FITNICARAGUA.ORG** to learn more.

adoption

To start off, let's set the baseline for our conversations about **adoption**. In particular, I want to highlight five Biblical references to **adoption**, to set the stage, so to speak, in regards to why anyone should even adopt at all. Throughout this week, I hope you'll see how **adoption** is near and dear to God's own heart, and something he models for us repeatedly in scripture.

But I'm already adopting, so I know all of this!

I can promise you that at some point in the process you will forget.

Maybe it'll happen because you're separated from the rest of your family during an extended fostering period abroad.

Maybe it'll pop up in the moment you realize just how profoundly your life has changed... so much so that a portion of you longs to "go back."

Maybe it'll occur when you've hit your limit for the number of times you can hear a child scream, *You're not my mother!*

Or maybe it'll simply bubble to the surface during a rare quiet moment when you're curled up with a book and realized just how infrequent those personal moments are...

However it happens, *it will happen.* And when it does, I want the scripture highlighted in this book to take over any doubts or fears that might otherwise seep in.

Finally, brothers, whatever is true, whatever is honorable, whatever is just, whatever is pure, whatever is lovely, whatever is commendable, if there is any excellence, if there is anything worthy of praise, think about these things.
—Philippians 4:8 (ESV)

DAY 1 //adoption

Now a man from the house of Levi went and took as his wife a Levite woman. The woman conceived and bore a son, and when she saw that he was a fine child, she hid him three months. When she could hide him no longer, she took for him a basket made of bulrushes and daubed it with bitumen and pitch. She put the child in it and placed it among the reeds by the river bank. And his sister stood at a distance to know what would be done to him.

Now the daughter of Pharaoh came down to bathe at the river, while her young women walked beside the river. She saw the basket among the reeds and sent her servant woman, and she took it. When she opened it, she saw the child, and behold, the baby was crying. She took pity on him and said, "This is one of the Hebrews' children." Then his sister said to Pharaoh's daughter, "Shall I go and call you a nurse from the Hebrew women to nurse the child for you?" And Pharaoh's daughter said to her, "Go." So the girl went and called the child's mother. And Pharaoh's daughter said to her, "Take this child away and nurse him for me, and I will give you your wages." So the woman took the child and nursed him. When the child grew older, she brought him to Pharaoh's daughter, and he became her son. She named him Moses, "Because," she said, "I drew him out of the water." —Exodus 2:1-10 (ESV)

You don't have to read very far into the Bible to encounter the first **adoption** story. The second chapter of Exodus tells about a woman who loved her child so much that she gave him up. If that sounds like a line you've heard before but thought too good to be true... consider that she knew Pharaoh had ordered all Hebrew male infants to be killed. She knew her child faced a very real danger from a very real threat.

If I were in her shoes, I would have been desperate to save my son. Rather than risk her son's life, she choose to give him away, in the hopes that his heritage might not be the cause of his death...

I find it particularly interesting that this **adoption** is not even about a traditional orphan, at least not in the sense that most of us think. This child had living parents who could not care for him in the way he needed. So he was given up. *For another mother to love.* And God blessed them all in the process.

Shockingly, the mother who previously hid her son and sent him floating down the Nile River was later asked to nurse him by the woman who found him! Moses' bio mom (to borrow the phrase from our generation) didn't know if she'd ever see her son again, but God gave her the gift of precious time to safely love and care for her son, before he was eventually **adopted** by Pharaoh's own daughter (of all people).

The woman who raised Moses may not have known the circumstances surrounding his initial months of life, but clearly that didn't matter. His appearance very likely marked him as one destined to die according to her own father's decree, but she chose to accept him as her own anyway. *I don't even want to consider what might have happened to Moses had Pharaoh's daughter not rescued him from the Nile...*

Do you recall what became of that child? Well, he was highly educated by the best of the best and treated as a royal son.[1] He likely spent 40 years being groomed by the Egyptian elite in the law, languages, math, and religion. Clearly Pharaoh's daughter both loved and protected this child. And out of that love, Moses grew up to be one of God's most faithful servants, even writing the first five books of the Bible. *Not too shabby for an **adopted** kid.*

*Father, when we are tempted to consider **adoption** as sub-par, remind us of your faithful servant Moses, who was loved first by you, next by the mother who birthed him and gave him up, and finally by the mother who clutched him from the river just in your perfect timing. Thank you for giving us this beautiful picture of **adoption**.*

1   HTTPS://WWW.BIBLEGATEWAY.COM/RESOURCES/ALL-WOMEN-BIBLE/PHARAOH-8217-S-DAUGHTER

DAY 2 //adoption

Now there was a Jew in Susa the citadel whose name was Mordecai, the son of Jair, son of Shimei, son of Kish, a Benjaminite, who had been carried away from Jerusalem among the captives carried away with Jeconiah king of Judah, whom Nebuchadnezzar king of Babylon had carried away. He was bringing up Hadassah, that is Esther, the daughter of his uncle, for she had neither father nor mother. The young woman had a beautiful figure and was lovely to look at, and when her father and her mother died, Mordecai took her as his own daughter. —Esther 2:5-7 (ESV)

Many of us are quite familiar with the story of Esther. (Can I admit it is my favorite Veggie Tales movie?) In fact, when asked to quickly name a Biblical character with whom I identify, Esther is high on the list.

After all, she was an unlikely candidate for queen. While Scripture tells us she was beautiful, it also tells us she had lost both parents at an early age. And it wasn't as if she was of royal lineage in Persia... she was Jewish! She was **adopted** by her cousin, who cared for her as if she were his own daughter.

Against all odds, Esther—the **adopted** child of Mordecai—became queen.

As wonderful as that might have been, trouble was brewing for the Jews. The King's advisors came up with a scheme to get rid of the Jews. When Mordecai told Esther the news, she didn't know what to do. Her cousin wanted her to plead their case in front of the King, but Esther was worried. She certainly didn't feel like any sort of savior for the Jews...

But her cousin reminded her in Chapter 4, verses 13-14, *"Do not think to yourself that in the king's palace you will escape any more than all the other Jews. For if you keep silent at this time, relief and deliverance will rise for the Jews from another place, but you and your father's house will perish. And who knows whether you have not come to the kingdom for such a time as this?"*

Whenever I am feeling inadequate, scared, insignificant, or completely unprepared for a particular situation—related to parenting, ministry, work, or just life—I find a lot of encouragement in Mordecai's pep talk to Esther.

And in those dark moments, I often consider what Mordecai's response *to me* might be... "Don't think that you're in this situation for no reason! God doesn't waste anything. If you sit around and do nothing, God will work out his plan through someone else, but you'll still suffer. Have you considered that you might have been put in this position specifically so God can use it for his glory?"

No matter what your **adopted** child has come from and no matter how she ended up in your family, God loves you both. He put her into your family to work out his plan. It may not always feel comfortable, or safe, or pleasant, but that doesn't change the fact that *God is good.* And, if you allow him, he wants to use your child and your family to show his glory.

Father God, thank you for the amazing ways you use each one of us, regardless of where we came from or whether we feel adequate, to further your Kingdom and declare your glory.

DAY 3 //adoption

The first two days of this week, we looked at **adoption** stories from the Old Testament. Today, I want to switch over to the New Testament, to look at yet another Biblical example of **adoption**.

Scripture tells us in the first chapter of Matthew that Jesus was conceived within a virgin. While Mary was engaged to Joseph at the time, Jesus was not the biological product of that union.

Now the birth of Jesus Christ took place in this way. When his mother Mary had been betrothed to Joseph, before they came together she was found to be with child from the Holy Spirit. (v. 18 ESV)

Step outside of the Biblical story here for a moment, to consider what that scenario might look like in your own life. You are planning a wedding to one man, but suddenly become pregnant with someone else's child.

This is where my teenage daughter would say... *uh, awkward!*

And her husband Joseph, being a just man and unwilling to put her to shame, resolved to divorce her quietly. (v. 19 ESV)

But God had other plans. He sent an angel to talk Joseph out of leaving... to convince him to "adopt" Jesus and raise him as his own.

When Joseph woke from sleep, he did as the angel of the Lord commanded him: he took his wife, but knew her not until she had given birth to a son. And he called his name Jesus. (v. 25 ESV)

I know this nativity story well. But up until recently, I hadn't really stopped to consider Joseph's earthly **adoption** of Jesus. It strikes me that God could have done this whole thing way differently. He could have placed Jesus in Mary's womb *before* she was engaged, to remove any chance of shame on Joseph. But then, Mary would have been left alone and the child would likely have grown up without an earthly father. Or, Jesus could have been conceived immediately after the wedding, so Joseph wouldn't have any chance of abandoning the child. The problem with that scenario is that many would doubt the truth of the virgin birth.

Clearly God purposed this conception to happen at just the right moment, so his plan could be gloriously revealed. And how amazing that this plan included the **adoption** *of the Christ child* by an earthly parent.

Heavenly Father, thank you for giving us yet another example of Biblical **adoption**... *of your own Son, of all people! Strengthen us as we resolve to follow your commands and live out your will for our lives.*

DAY 4 //adoption

Focusing on these five Biblical accounts this week helps us recognize how positively **adoption** is referenced in Scripture. For the final two days, we move from the physical **adoption** of Moses, Esther, and Jesus by non-biological parents, to our own spiritual **adoption** by God.

Today let's look at how **adoption** is modeled in the book of Galatians. In his letter to the church of Galatia, Paul is careful to remind us, *"You are all sons of God through faith in Christ Jesus."* (Galatians 3:26 NASB)

And he doesn't stop there.

"But when the fullness of time had come, God sent forth his Son, born of woman, born under the law, to redeem those who were under the law, so that we might receive **adoption** *as sons."* (Galatians 4:4-5 ESV)

Paul initially said we were all "sons" of God, but then he describes each one of us as "**adopted**" children. In our culture, adding the "**adopted**" tagline doesn't always have a positive connotation, does it? But Paul seems to use the two words—sons and **adopted**—almost interchangeably. And then he outlines what it means to be either one: *"since you are a son, God has made you also an heir."* (v. 7)

This, my friends, is a game-changer.

The word *heir* is typically defined as "a person legally entitled to the property or rank of another on that person's death." Synonyms include successor and beneficiary. In naming us—his **adopted** children—as *heirs*, Christ passed all of his wealth on to us. Not only that, he designated us as beneficiaries of his entire inheritance.

All of it.

It doesn't matter where we were born, or to whom. He doesn't care what terrible things we've done in the past or where those decisions leave us. He only knows that he loves us. Completely. Utterly. And without fail. In fact, he loves us so much that he would give up *everything* for us—his heirs—just so that we might truly live.

Pretty amazing inheritance for us "**adopted**" kids, isn't it? And what a beautiful picture of how we are to love each of our own children, no matter where they came from.

*Father, thank you. Thank you for **adopting** us and making us heirs to your kingdom. Thank you for loving us enough to send your own Son to the cross, for the sake of our inheritance.*

DAY 5 //adoption

Pure and genuine religion in the sight of God the Father means caring for orphans and widows in their distress and refusing to let the world corrupt you. —James 1:27 (NLT)

I remember the first time my husband and I talked about what this verse meant to our family. It happened on our honeymoon (yes, I realize that was probably a silly time for us to finally talk about kids!). Anyway, we both agreed **adoption** or orphan care would play into our family structure at some point, simply because God commanded it.

Fast forward a decade or so, and we started considering **adopting** from Nicaragua. During a trip there, we proudly told a missionary about our plans to "save a child." He shocked us with his response: "You're not ready for that."

Excuse me! Did this guy even know me?

He suggested we should first become foster parents in our home community for a while, so we could really get a handle on what *caring for orphans without letting the world corrupt you* means. Eighteen months later, as we were knee deep in the midst of fostering two previously homeless teenage girls, we finally started to understand.

This caring for orphans business isn't just about us "saving kids." Of course many children are saved from physical harm in the process of **adoption**, but it's so much more than that.

And that portion about not letting the world corrupt us? Apparently James knew exactly what he was talking about when he included that tidbit.

Caring for other peoples' children is messy work. After having their world turned upside down—and losing part of their identity—they often aren't as "appreciative" as we might want. The whole experience can be challenging, frustrating, and exhausting, for both parent and child.

It's enough to make us bitter, jaded, and maybe even a tiny bit regretful. *What was that James said about the world corrupting us?*

True religion—the stuff that God wants us to focus on—isn't merely caring for orphans, but doing it in such a way that we don't let all of the darkness and sin and frustration of this world break us. It means caring for these children so that they know they are heirs not only to *all* the blessings of our earthly family, but also to the great inheritance of our heavenly one.

Precious Savior, I am so tempted by the world. Thank you for providing your Word, to strengthen me so I can better care for each of your children.

self-care

Any parent knows that raising kids is a full-time—and then some—job. As we run from one thing to the next, it is common to sometimes feel like we are barely holding it together. In those moments, it seems like one wrong move could send us toppling over the edge.

We cannot adequately care for our children if we aren't also caring for ourselves. This is not to say we should place our own needs in front of our child's, but rather that we mustn't ignore our own needs in caring for others. As moms, we need to balance the needs of our children with our own, to ensure the whole family is well cared for, supported, and loved. This week, **MELISSA CORKUM** uses a variety of scripture references to identify ways in which we can better **care for our body, mind, and soul**, to then care for our loved ones.

DAY 1 //self-care

You have searched me, Lord, and you know me. You know when I sit and when I rise; you perceive my thoughts from afar. You discern my going out and my lying down; you are familiar with all my ways. Before a word is on my tongue you, Lord, know it completely. You hem me in behind and before, and you lay your hand upon me. —Psalm 139:1-5 (NIV)

Shortly after we brought home our son from Korea in 2009, we realized that the parenting techniques we used on our bio kids fell tragically short of meeting the needs of a child from a hard place. Fortunately, we became immersed in a therapeutic method called trust-based parenting[1]. While the principles outlined in trust-based parenting have literally saved our family from disruption and destruction, they are H A R D to carry out daily, requiring an immense amount of parental patience and compassion.

In the lowest part of our journey, God was gracious enough to show me that the missing piece was my **self-care**. Our children constantly rely on us to keep their endless anxieties at bay and regulate their emotions along with all the other typical food/shelter requirements. This requires us to be "on" all the time that we're with them. This is an impossibly tall order that can only be fulfilled if we take the time to care for ourselves spiritually, mentally, and physically. After all, we're only human, too.

As I gave myself permission to address my physical, emotional, and spiritual needs, the words that echoed in my spirit were, "*You are precious.*" (Isaiah 43:4 ESV)

I felt him reassuring me that being a "good" parent did not include detrimental self-sacrifice. Somewhere along the lines I had picked up a subconscious, self-imposed requirement that I should be physically present with my kids virtually every minute of the day. Ironically, boxing myself in like that had made me a grouchy, crabby mama who my kids really didn't want to be around anyway. I had falsely figured that to care for myself meant my kids would take a back seat and vice versa when, in truth, *we are all precious*. No back seat necessary.

Thank you, God, for being everywhere and knowing me so intimately. Search me and know my anxious thoughts and bring me peace. With the anxiety gone, help me to have eyes like you so I can see my children's and my preciousness as you see us.

---

1   Trust-based parenting equips parents with a holistic understanding of their child's needs and development while empowering them with the tools and strategies to effectively meet those needs, build trust, and help their child heal and grow. (HTTP://WWW.NCBI.NLM.NIH.GOV/PMC/ARTICLES/PMC3877861/)

DAY 2 //self-care

Be still and know that I am God; I will be exalted among the nations, I will be exalted in the earth. —Psalm 46:10 (NIV)

I spent years, to my detriment, trying to control what was going on, not just logistically, but emotionally in our house. I realized that I had asked God to bless our efforts to find the best nutrition plan, the most effective therapies, and everything else I had calculated that our kids needed to be "successful," but I was still holding out that I had some semblance of control over how things went. I believed we (with God's help, of course) could find the systems that would solve the depression, the closed-mindedness, the poor comprehension, the lack of social/emotional development, the anger, and the hurt. After all, that's why God put them here, right?

The phrase, "...or die trying" rang through my head. I was literally pouring my life into my kids, and they were either rejecting it or just letting it flow right past. There was almost no return on investment and my bank account was in the red.

Meanwhile, all my efforts were backfiring. The systems were creating chaos and the emptier my emotional bank became, the more I transformed into a person I didn't recognize–mean, nasty, spiteful, and resentful.

But God has called me to **care for myself** so I can love my family well and leave the details—and the outcomes—to him. I won't lie. This is much easier said than done.

Be still and know that I am God.

He reminded me of a silent retreat I attended the year before. I experienced peace and healing there where I least expected it. I didn't have to run around looking for it, it found me once I was quiet and still.

Sure I continue my due diligence to advocate for my children and take advantages of services that fit in with our lifestyle. However, they do not NEED every offering out there. I also search for resources with a new sense of peace, void of the frantic sense of urgency that our kids' success and healing depend on those resources. Remember that you, and your children, are precious to God. *You do not love your kiddos more than he does!* Give yourself permission to let it go (whatever "it" is for you) and take some time to rest in his care.

Help me to trust in you and be still, oh God. Remind me often that you are BIG enough to handle the seemingly endless challenges—even if we don't find the perfect therapist.

DAY 3 //self-care

Do not judge, or you too will be judged. For in the same way you judge others, you will be judged, and with the measure you use, it will be measured to you. Why do you look at the speck of sawdust in your brother's eye and pay no attention to the plank in your own eye? How can you say to your brother, 'Let me take the speck out of your eye,' when all the time there is a plank in your own eye?

You hypocrite, first take the plank out of your own eye, and then you will see clearly to remove the speck from your brother's eye. Do not give dogs what is sacred; do not throw your pearls to pigs. If you do, they may trample them under their feet, and turn and tear you to pieces. —Matthew 7:1-6 (NIV)

The most powerful statement that propelled me to return to self-care was, "*I cannot change my child but I can change me.*" My head knew this, but when it made its way into my heart, it was transformational.

I can't change the manipulative, self-centered, self-protective behavior, but I can look to God to help me understand why it bothers me so much. Every parent has different "buttons," and you can bet your child knows exactly which ones you have. Take some time for self-reflection and ask God to heal all those past hurts so you can be emotionally available for your kids.

I can't change the meanness, but I can view it through Jesus' eyes and see the scared child who is lashing out to protect herself. When our feelings are hurt, we often are mean right back. Take time to fill up your emotional tank so you can give grace, mercy, and forgiveness without reserve.

I can't change the irresponsibility and the developmental mismatches, but I can take on a servant's heart to find joy in serving them… even when there's a temptation to render judgment, or to "teach them a lesson" because they should know better.

I can't change the attitude, but I can slow my life down, taking time to validate the emotions behind it. Often, I volley back with just as much attitude because I'm overstressed and tired. I owe it to my kids to rest up enough so I have the energy to help them find their appropriate voice *without losing mine in the process.*

Take the time to **address your emotional health**. Re-center yourself and cling tightly to the steadfast love of God. That way when the emotional storms come, you can stay grounded instead of being swept away in them.

God, show me the depth of my sinfulness so that I may not be so quick to judge the actions of those around me, but instead show compassion as you have shown me.

DAY 4 //self-care

I thank my God every time I remember you. In all my prayers for all of you, I always pray with joy because of your partnership in the gospel from the first day until now, being confident of this, that he who began a good work in you will carry it on to completion until the day of Christ Jesus.

It is right for me to feel this way about all of you, since I have you in my heart and, whether I am in chains or defending and confirming the gospel, all of you share in God's grace with me. God can testify how I long for all of you with the affection of Christ Jesus. And this is my prayer: that your love may abound more and more in knowledge and depth of insight, so that you may be able to discern what is best and may be pure and blameless for the day of Christ, filled with the fruit of righteousness that comes through Jesus Christ—to the glory and praise of God. —Philippians 1:3-11 (NIV)

In the midst of the emotional chaos that often reigns in our house, it is easy to lose sight of God's promises and the truths about how precious our kiddos are, how God has called us, and how he is faithful to finish the work he has started. Protecting our thought-life is of great importance if we are to endure in this life.

With three kids who were adopted at older ages into a foreign culture, we are often helping them navigate feelings of discouragement and defeatism. Building confidence in them is a constant battle. One of our family activities is Tae Kwon Do, a Korean martial art. Our instructor often tells us that we are not allowed to utter the words, "I can't." Only, "I'll try" or, better, "I can!"

"You can't have confidence unless you have confident words," he encourages us, and I find myself repeating this admonishment to my kids.

One day, God impressed on me that I also had the power to **transform my mind**. I felt convicted to seek God's promises, using them to push out the discouragement and doubt that can creep into my soul. As I bathe my mind and thoughts in truth, I find that my perspective changes for the better, and I feel more equipped to love my children well.

I invite you to meditate on God's truths. Repeat them often and out loud today and in the days to come. Let your mind be renewed and may God's peace be with you today. Remember that he has begun a good work in your family and he will carry it on to completion.

God, may the words of my mouth and the meditations of my heart be from You. Protect me from the lies Satan tries to plant in our minds.

DAY 5 //self-care

Jesus went throughout Galilee, teaching in their synagogues, proclaiming the good news of the kingdom, and healing every disease and sickness among the people. News about him spread all over Syria, and people brought to him all who were ill with various diseases, those suffering severe pain, the demon-possessed, those having seizures, and the paralyzed; and he healed them. Large crowds from Galilee, the Decapolis, Jerusalem, Judea and the region across the Jordan followed him. —Matthew 4:23-25 (NIV)

From the blind to the lame to the diseased, Jesus' ministry was marked by caring not only for the spiritual and emotional needs of the people, but also the physical ones. His example underscores the importance of taking care of ourselves, from watching what we put into our bodies to how we keep them running well.

Nutrition played a huge role in stabilizing our little guy from Korea. Then, soon after bringing our older kids home, we realized that movement was a healthy, non-invasive way to address depression as well as anxious energy. Since older kids are more "do as I do" as opposed to just "do what I say," my husband and I also found ourselves exercising more.

As a result, I was amazed to discover how strong the mind-body connection is. Jesus certainly knew what he was doing! As I've put **caring for my body** near the top of my priority list to feel physical well, I've found my mind and spirit follow suit. While there seldom seems time to properly care for our bodies, we have a responsibility to care for God's temple well.

Do you not know that your bodies are temples of the Holy Spirit, who is in you, whom you have received from God? You are not your own; you were bought at a price. Therefore honor God with your bodies. —1 Cor. 6:19-20 (NIV)

When our earthly vessels are in tip-top shape, we are in a better place to live out God's calling in our lives. Whether you find yourself wading through the drudgery of paperwork, twiddling your thumbs while you wait, or in the post-placement trenches, challenge yourself to move more, drink more water, and take steps to improve your nutrition. In addition, schedule a daily period of "down time" to re-energize. Maybe you take a walk, read, or pray; the actual activity doesn't matter as long as you are without demands and distractions.

This passage is also a reminder to me that we serve a God who is powerful enough to heal us physically, emotionally, and spiritually. No matter where you are on your journey, remember to care for yourself so you can live out his calling on your life well.

Father, I pray for your peace, protection, and healing on my family. Thank you for providing us with our earthly bodies, made in your own image. Give us the strength to endure the challenges before us.

faith

This week, **CARRIE LEISTER** walks us through her journey of faith, encompassing ten years of adoption in Nicaragua. She draws wisdom from Hebrews 11 and Psalms 37 and 113 to remind each of us about the glorious rewards of expectant **faith** in Christ Jesus.

SCRIPTURE FOCUS

He gives the barren woman a home, making her the joyous mother of children.
—Psalm 113:9 (ESV)

Delight yourself in the Lord, and he will give you the desires of your heart.
—Psalm 37:4 (ESV)

Now faith is the substance of things hoped for, the evidence of things not seen.
—Hebrews 11:1 (NKJV)

DAY 1 //faith

*Now **faith** is the substance of things hoped for, the evidence of things not seen.*
—Hebrews 11:1

As I listened to the missionaries speak about homeless children, some as young as four-and five-years-old, living under a bridge near Lake Managua, my heart broke. I vividly remember the description they gave of the little helpless souls collecting cardboard and other recyclables to exchange for a jar of glue. I was horrified to learn this addictive substance is commonly used—even by children—in Nicaragua, to kill the pain of hunger and loneliness.

For two years I had been fully engaged in working with these missionaries on short-term medical mission teams to Mexico. My life was completely transformed by those short-term trips but this was more than I could bear. I silently cried in my heart "God, please let me go to Nicaragua. Even if only once. *Maybe I could help one child.*"

It was a simple prayer, only heard by God… a hope I gave over to him that day. As I listened to the tragic tales, of homeless and helpless souls suffering in loneliness, I believe God allowed me to feel a tiny piece of his pain for the children of Nicaragua. He gave me eyes to see and ears to hear the cries of orphans amidst the darkness of our world. And he provided me with an opportunity to have **faith** that I might one day offer some ray of hope to one of those children.

As South African missionary, Andrew Murray, once said, *"**Faith** expects from God what is beyond all expectation."* Throughout our **faith** journey, God desires to teach us about placing our complete trust in him, with expectant hope. He desires that we rejoice in the wonderful unexpected, as we embrace the beautiful truth that his unseen plan is infinitely better than we could ever imagine.

The words of those missionaries, and my subsequent prayer—from the depths of my heart—began a ten-year journey for us in the Central American country of Nicaragua. God knew, as I prayed that brief, desperate prayer, that so many things were unseen to me. He also knew the blessings that would abound. Adoption and so much more!

*Father help me embrace your gift of **faith**. Fill me with a hope that is from your heart. Let me rest knowing and trusting that the things you have in my future, yet unseen are beautiful. Amen.*

DAY 2 //faith

As my physician handed me a prescription for the infertility medication, I asked God "is this really what you have for our family?" Peace is not what I felt in that moment. And should I be taking something that has a long list of potential side effects when I will be boarding a plane for Nicaragua in two weeks?

God had answered my unspoken prayer from two years prior. My husband and I were invited to join a medical team, to serve in Nicaragua. It was a good distraction after a year and a half of waiting for a pregnancy and month after month of disappointment.

Now, with several medical tests behind us and no clear answer as to why we were not conceiving, it was as though God was telling me to *rest in him*. If pregnancy were God's plan for us, then certainly he was able to bring that about in our lives, right? I was going to trust him to bring to pass the verse that had given me so much hope.

He gives the barren woman a home, making her the joyous mother of children. —Psalm 113:9

There was a part of my heart that was willing to surrender and, in **faith,** say that I would trust him with the future of our family. For now, the full surrender would have to wait. I wanted to put it on the back burner, because I was going to Nicaragua!

I love medical missions; they ignite a place in my heart like nothing else, so I thought it would be the perfect distraction from thinking about having a family. I have always felt a nearness to the heart of God when I serve in Central America. I counted it a gift from God that he would allow me such a privilege to serve him in this way.

When God says he gives us the desires of our hearts, (Psalm 37:4) I know he gave me this trip as an answer to my unspoken prayer and desire to go to Nicaragua once and help a child. I could not have imagined what God was about to do in my life. *"Now faith is the substance of things hoped for, the evidence of things not seen."* (Hebrews 11:1)

I praise you, God, this day for the gifts you give, the seen and unseen. I thank you for the desires you place in our hearts and the blessings that come as we journey through receiving those desires. Amen.

DAY 3 //faith

We arrived late, in the darkness of night so my first glimpse of Nicaragua was limited. The view my first morning was stunning, it was green and lush. From the porch of our team facility I could see a volcano in the distance. I was in love! We worshiped together in the morning with plans to spend the afternoon at the children's home next-door distributing Christmas gifts.

As I stepped up to the front door of the children's home, a little boy was staring out the window... one child. Here was one precious boy saved from the streets and in a loving place. Thank God for places like this. We were given a tour and our first stop was the nursery. As a hopeful mother this caused a bit of pain in my heart. One by one the babies and toddlers were awakened from their naps, rubbing their eyes, unsure of the visitors. One sweet toddler girl stood out... she had a lavender dress with a white, slightly torn collar. Her dark eye and dark curly hair, pulled up into a cute ponytail on top, instantly pulled at my heart.

Our team enjoyed the afternoon as we gave out shoe boxes filled with wonderful gifts. The kids were ecstatic and had such fun playing with their new treasures. All day the quiet, curly haired toddler found her way in my lap. I couldn't leave her if I tried. It just felt right. Everyday I would arrive "home" to our team facility and spend my free time with her.

I spent the week ministering with my team to the sick, traveling the countryside and soaking in all that Nicaragua had for me but my mind and heart was consumed with just one child. It was as though the pain of infertility began to fade and become a blessing as I realized God had been saving my husband and me for this very moment, this very child.

Delight yourself in the Lord, and he will give you the desires of your heart.
—Psalm 37:4

As we inquired about her, doors began to open, and the word *no* was never uttered. Adoption was in our future and hers. My desire to help one child was being answered, but in a way I never expected. My desire for a family was also being answered. Oh the joys of long-ago promises being fulfilled.

Leaving Nicaragua was painful, but I had a mission now.... adoption.

*Heavenly Father, help me to have **faith** and to trust you with the desires of my heart. You are the giver of good gifts to your children. Let me rest in your perfect timing for my life.*

DAY 4 //faith

In Hebrews 11:8 it says of Abraham that: "*He went out, not knowing whither he went.*" There are times in our life when God calls us to step out into the great unknown. Nicaraguan adoption was completely unknown to me and most everyone I talked to during that time.

I was smitten, in love with a beautiful, brown-eyed baby girl in Nicaragua. I knew in my heart she was my daughter. But now what? So many things were unclear and many days I sat down and cried. God I know you didn't bring me to this child to allow me to lose her over things like applications, background checks, fingerprints, translations, and residency requirements.

In those initial stages I felt alone, very alone. Oswald Chambers writes in *My Utmost for His Highest* when speaking of faith, "**Faith** never knows where it is being led, but it loves and knows the one who is leading. It is a life of **faith**, not of intellect and reason, but a life of knowing who makes us go." Through this time of paperwork preparation and wading through a process on my own I learned to cry out to God for direction and help. And, in time, direction came through many different resources. I had to step out in **faith**, one document, one phone call, one process at a time, reminding myself that he was the one leading.

Oswald Chambers goes on to say, "The life of **faith** is not a life of mounting up with wings, but a life of walking and not fainting." Our first adoption lasted almost five years. And it definitely was a journey of walking and not fainting.

I completed that first round of paperwork and many, many other rounds. My husband and I were blessed to adopt that beautiful brown-eyed toddler. And then we met another beautiful brown eyed, curly haired toddler girl. She is now a part of our family as well.

I count the journey of our adoptions as a gift... a gift that drew me so close to my Savior, and the gift of not one child but two beautiful girls that fill our home with love and laughter. It was a **faith** journey that took me somewhere I didn't know I could go. The gift continues as God allows us to work in the beautiful country of Nicaragua.

Oswald Chambers adds that "The final stage in the life of **faith** is attainment of character."

*God, lead us in our journey of **faith**, that we will endure and continue as you transform our character to be like you.*

DAY 5 //faith

Now faith is the substance of things hoped for, the evidence of things not seen.
—Hebrews 11:1

Unseen and unexpected, that is what the prayer for one child brought into my life. God gave the gift of two daughters. He also answered with the faces of many more.

The adoption journey is a huge step of **faith** and once anyone says yes to it, the unexpected will happen. Through the course of our ten-year adoption journey God opened the door for our family to serve him continually in Nicaragua through short mission teams. We love to take teams to share medical care, school supplies, sports ministry, and any other gifts that God gives. Not only has it been an incredible blessing for the people of Nicaragua, but it has been life changing for the team members that have had the opportunity to go. God continues to open door after door to allow this ministry to continue.

In March of 2014, during the early morning hours before heading out to minister with a medical team, I was once again reading the verse from Psalm 113 but this time in the Amplified translation, *"He makes the barren woman to be a homemaker and a joyful mother of spiritual children. Praise the Lord!"*

Immediately I was reminded of an overwhelming moment earlier that week. I was leading a large group of children in a fun, Spanish version of *Alelujah, Praise Ye the Lord.* They were so happy and their faces filled with joy. As the song progressed they moved in closer, until they surrounded our team and me. I felt as though I was receiving a big hug from all 50 kids. It was a special moment filled with an incredible sense of unconditional love. As I reflected, God was showing me the magnitude of what he can do with one prayer multiplied by his word and power. The picture of that moment, the verse, the past ten years, and my two daughters all came together in my mind to signify the enormity of God.

In my infertility, God blessed me with a family and so much more. He enlarged my heart and taught me lessons on **faith**. He gave me "spiritual children" whose faces leave an imprint on my heart each and every time I visit them. And it never gets old. This world can give us happiness but God gives treasures in life that I call true joy.

*Heavenly Father, help me to trust you, because you are worthy to be trusted. You alone give good gifts. In **faith** I will rest in you for my future and the future of my family. Amen*

barrenness

Many families enter into the adoption process due to **barrenness**. Regardless of the path God brings us along in order to meet and parent our children, his mercies and promises remain. This week, **CAROLINE BAILEY** shares about how God used Hannah's story to encourage and guide her as she walked her adoption path.

SCRIPTURE FOCUS //1 SAMUEL 1: 1-16 (NIV)

There was a certain man from Ramathaim, a Zuphite from the hill country of Ephraim, whose name was Elkanah son of Jeroham, the son of Elihu, the son of Tohu, the son of Zuph, an Ephraimite. He had two wives; one was called Hannah and the other Peninnah. Peninnah had children, but Hannah had none.

Year after year this man went up from his town to worship and sacrifice to the Lord Almighty at Shiloh, where Hophni and Phinehas, the two sons of Eli, were priests of the Lord. Whenever the day came for Elkanah to sacrifice, he would give portions of the meat to his wife Peninnah and to all her sons and daughters. But to Hannah he gave a double portion because he loved her, and the Lord had closed her womb. Because the Lord had closed Hannah's womb, her rival kept provoking her in order to irritate her. This went on year after year. Whenever Hannah went up to the house of the Lord, her rival provoked her till she wept and would not eat. Her husband Elkanah would say to her, "Hannah, why are you weeping? Why don't you eat? Why are you downhearted? Don't I mean more to you than ten sons?"

Once when they had finished eating and drinking in Shiloh, Hannah stood up. Now Eli the priest was sitting on his chair by the doorpost of the Lord's house. In her deep anguish Hannah prayed to the Lord, weeping bitterly. And she made a vow, saying, "Lord Almighty, if you will only look on your servant's misery and remember me, and not forget your servant but give her a son, then I will give him to the Lord for all the days of his life, and no razor will ever be used on his head."

As she kept on praying to the Lord, Eli observed her mouth. Hannah was praying in her heart, and her lips were moving but her voice was not heard. Eli thought she was drunk, and said to her, "How long are you going to stay drunk? Put away your wine."

"Not so, my lord," Hannah replied, "I am a woman who is deeply troubled. I have not been drinking wine or beer; I was pouring out my soul to the Lord. Do not take your servant for a wicked woman; I have been praying here out of my great anguish and grief."

DAY 1 //*barrenness*

"When you can find a purpose bigger than you, you can persevere through anything." —Tyrone Flowers

This quote speaks volumes to me now, but back before my home was filled with children... not so much. It isn't easy growing up infertile. There were moments when I sought anything to give me some measure of reason. Finding purpose in **barrenness** seemed like an everlasting quest.

After all, even if the purpose was found, the barrenness would remain.

I think back and hear my Mother's words, *"You can accomplish anything if you just put your heart to it."* I witnessed her own gumption to get up each day, and raise a daughter who might never raise a daughter.

Just as I was starting to develop into adolescence, I underwent an emergency hysterectomy. At eleven-years-old, this was a major blow to my self-esteem. Although I survived it, and went about living a seemingly typical American life, I immediately became mightily aware of the vast difference between myself and the other girls.

*Despite the normalcy, **barrenness** remained.* Comparison set in. Feelings of inadequacy, confusion, and loneliness become prevalent. **Barrenness** seemed to be this faceless, hopeless, and life-depriving adjective for my life; at least, until I was met heart-to-heart with the Lord. Despite my own set of failed attempts to make it all right, and my rebellious spirit, our Father in Heaven has drawn me nearer and nearer to him.

Forget the former things; do not dwell on the past. See, I am doing a new thing! Now it springs up; do you not perceive it? I am making a way in the wilderness and streams in the wasteland. —Isaiah 43:18-19 (NIV)

Do you dwell on the past while also worrying about the future? Do you long for a living, breathing answer to the pain of the years? *Be still, sweet sister.* The Lord is making a way through this wilderness of pain you are traversing. He is supplying life-giving streams in the wasteland. You crave newness and refreshment. Forget the former things. Do not dwell on what has been. Pray with hopeful anticipation of what is to come. Anticipate the spring. Do not fret the wilderness. Stand tall in faith that the very God who breathed life itself into existence is on your side. He hears your prayers. He walks beside your woeful ways. He will deliver. He will not forsake you. *He never has.*

Dear Heavenly Father, I feel your presence in my life, but sometimes the pain seems to want to take me over. I'm feeling inadequate, lonely, as though the only song I'll ever sing is one filled with sorrow. Dear Father, consume my thoughts with ones that are not of pain, but instead, of the hope that is to come. Make my way through this wilderness. Guide me through the streams of this wasteland and fill my soul with a newness that can only come from you. Thank you, Father, for your ever-present quenching of my thirst.

DAY 2 //barrenness

We learn in this week's scripture focus that Hannah was full of trouble... deep trouble. Her agony was all encompassing. It must have felt that the entire world was on her shoulders. I don't know about you, but I feel such a kindred connection to Hannah. With each passing year, it seems I have appreciated her faith and hope, more and more.

Barren and longing for a child, in a time of life on Earth that was not anywhere near where we are in understanding infertility and barrenness, must have been an incredibly difficult landscape to navigate. *I wonder how inadequate she must have felt.* I wonder how many moments in her life she sat up in the night, crying, and pleading to her Heavenly Father to fulfill that deepest longing of her life.

We know how the story of Hannah unfolded. We know that our God answered her prayers, and blessed her with a son. We rejoice while reading about her life. Her life, lived many years ago, still provides comfort to women around the world. It still speaks of the power of God.

What does Hannah's story say to you? Are you full of trouble? Is your agony all-encompassing? Do you feel inadequate?

Inadequacy is something I struggled with throughout the years. *Infertility and **barrenness** have a way of leading us down that path, doesn't it?*

Be still, sweet sister. Be still. The same Lord who listened while Hannah wailed also hears you. He sees you in your moments of weakness. He is near you in your times of despair. Draw near to him when you feel as though you are lesser than others in this world.

God heard Hannah's cry. He understood her longing, and he responded with an answer that has led many barren women to a place of hope for generations.

What does Hannah's story say to you? Are you full of trouble? Is your agony all-encompassing? Do you feel inadequate? Say these words: "My hope is in the Lord. For when you are near me, I am enough. I am not inadequate."

Dear Heavenly Father, I do not always understand your ways. I read the story of Hannah, and I am reminded of your goodness, but sometimes, Father, I do not respond in ways that lighten my path. I feel so inadequate at times that I do not put on a full armor of you. Father, help me to see you in all of this. Lift up my head, Lord. Lead me to that place of reckoning where my faults, troubles, and agonies are met with the sustenance of you. Thank you, Father, for answering Hannah's prayer. Thank you, Father, in advance for answering mine.

DAY 3 //barrenness

I've read this week's Scripture so many times that I could probably recite it by heart. However, just when I think I understand it or no longer can be moved by it, another part becomes a testament that strikes close to home. In the story of Hannah, these are the words that cause me to pause and consider what life was like for her, and for the rest of us who are declared **barren**: *Because the Lord had closed Hannah's womb, her rival kept provoking her in order to irritate her. This went on year after year. Whenever Hannah went up to the house of the Lord, her rival provoked her till she wept and would not eat.*

Am I saying that we have been provoked like Hannah? I certainly hope not. However, there are moments when we catch the undesired attention of the rest of the baby-bearing world.

Baby showers and pregnancy announcements can bring up those awful feelings of comparing your worth to others. I've been there... that dreaded place... of feeling as though my worth was measured by other women.

Have you ever felt that way? Be still, sweet sister. Be still.

This is what the Lord says in Ephesians 2:10 (NIV): *For we are his workmanship, created in Christ Jesus for good works, which God prepared beforehand, that we should walk in them.* And in Psalm 138:8 (NIV): *The LORD will fulfill his purpose for me; your steadfast love, O LORD, endures forever. Do not forsake the work of your hands.*

In Matthew 10:29-31 (NIV), Jesus tells us, "*Are not two sparrows sold for a penny? Yet not one of them will fall to the ground outside your Father's care. And even the very hairs of your head are all numbered. So don't be afraid; you are worth more than many sparrows.*"

You are his workmanship. You were created in Christ for good works that he has prepared. He does not forsake you. Every fiber of your being has worth. Every single hair is counted. You are more than the sparrow. Your plight of **barrenness** and the scars that have been created along the way are all just a ripple in the ocean compared to your value to the One True King.

The very God who cast the waves upon the oceans, molded the mountains, sketched the landscape, and breathed life into the lungs of all creation, treasures **you** most of all.

Dear Heavenly Father, there are those moments when I look upon other women and all I do is compare myself to them. I compare my body, my intentions, and my worth. I think, "Maybe God wants them to be mothers more than me." And then, Father, I feel you wrap my heart with your Word. Father, pad my path to motherhood with the absence of comparison, but instead, with the excitement and hope that is only found in you. Help me to remember that I am a valued treasure upon the Earth to which you created.

DAY 4 //barrenness

Hannah was praying in her heart, and her lips were moving but her voice was not heard. —1 Samuel 1:13

Praying in our hearts, often while they are breaking, is something that many of us are quite familiar with. Like Hannah, our despair might not be understood or even recognized. It feels, at times, that our endless, dry walk of desperation for motherhood might just go on and on.

Sojourning through the desert can lead to restoration, even though there may be pain in the journey. Like Hannah, we begin to cry out to God, not only in our despair, but also in that resonating place of deep hope. *We begin to visualize our future with children.*

"For I know the plans I have for you," declares the LORD, "plans to prosper you and not to harm you, plans to give you hope and a future." —Jeremiah 29:11 (NIV)

Be still, sweet sister. Be still. The seeds of hope have already been planted in your heart. The promise of our Father flows throughout your life... even in the midst of **barrenness**. It sings to you, dances with you, and carries you on those darkest of days.

You are broken; yet, despite it, you are being pulled towards the brokenness of others in this world. You feel that tugging of your heart towards the least of these, the abused, the neglected, the abandoned and often forgotten children. The tug has led you to the brink of opening the door to adoption.

You think, "Adoption? Is this something I want to venture into? What if I don't get matched? What if the children go back to their birth parents? What if nothing works out?" And then, in the same breath that you are exhaling your deepest worries, you feel the Breath of God saying,

"Trust me. Follow me. Hold on to Me."

Say these words: "My hope is in the Lord, and not just the hope of a future for my life, but the hope of all who dwell on Earth."

*Dear Heavenly Father, I am beginning to feel you pull me towards something much bigger than myself. My **barrenness** was once thought of as a deficit in my life, but now Father, I am seeing it as a part of my story. Or better yet, your story in my life. Father, lead me to the ones to which you intend for me. I trust you through all of this, but I still need you to lighten my load, and lift my head. Father, you have promised to fill me with hope, and a future, and for this, I am so incredibly thankful.*

DAY 5 *Barrenness*

And she made a vow, saying, "Lord Almighty, if you will only look on your servant's misery and remember me, and not forget your servant but give her a son, then I will give him to the Lord for all the days of his life, and no razor will ever be used on his head." —1 Samuel 1:11

The story of Hannah is one that has stirred the hearts of many women throughout generations. Hannah, with hope on her heart and faith in her vision, asked the Lord to bless her with a son. In return, she promised to give him back to God.

How many of us have asked the same of God, and promised the same in return? How many Hannahs are out there, wondering, waiting, and finally reaping the joy of faithfulness?

I do not understand the ways of the Lord. They are often far too mysterious for me to wrap my head around. I do know this: The Lord hears us. He listens to us. He answers us. And, he does not allow us to escape his blessings.

He settles the childless woman in her home as a happy mother of children. Praise the LORD. —Psalm 113:9 (NIV)

Sweet sister, you are embarking on a mission to find the beating heart that God created for you. Another woman carried that little soul in her womb, but you have carried this child, your child, in your heart.

It has been a long journey, hasn't it?

There have been moments when your own thoughts nearly convinced you that it wasn't worth it. The paperwork, the expectations, and the heartbreaks along the way seemed overwhelming.

Be still, sweet sister. Be still. In your quest to be a mother, in those hollowed out moments where nothing seemed to make sense, and in the moments of being truly awakened to the least of these, you have realized that perhaps your life is not filled with **barrenness** at all.

Religion that God our Father accepts as pure and faultless is this: to look after orphans and widows in their distress and to keep oneself from being polluted by the world. —James 1:27 (NIV)

Say these words: "My hope is the Lord, but not just my hope. My life story, written by you, is unfolding before me."

Dear Heavenly Father, I am eager to explore the road that you are walking me down. I look in expectation to the day that I will hold the children you created for me. I have felt inadequate, confused, and lost in the struggle of comparison, but now, Father, now I am being filled with a courageous kind of love. And I rest in the assurance that I too was composed for the life of the little soul to which I pray for. Thank you, Lord, for pulling me out of the wasteland, and restoring me with the richness of your love.

Worry

Parenting is hard and adoptive moms often feel like failures. Sometimes it seems like no matter what we try, we can't get through to our children. Behaviors continue despite every attempt to correct them. The house is a mess all the time. We often **worry** about the future. How can we possibly accomplish the task of raising godly children? This week, **AMIE COOPER** focus on the topic of **worry** and how to combat anxious thoughts by focusing our minds on the work of Christ in our families.

SCRIPTURE FOCUS //PHILIPPIANS 4: 4-9 (NIV)

Rejoice in the Lord always. I will say it again: Rejoice! Let your gentleness be evident to all. The Lord is near. Do not be anxious about anything, but in every situation, by prayer and petition, with thanksgiving, present your requests to God. And the peace of God, which transcends all understanding, will guard your hearts and your minds in Christ Jesus.

Finally, brothers and sisters, whatever is true, whatever is noble, whatever is right, whatever is pure, whatever is lovely, whatever is admirable—if anything is excellent or praiseworthy—think about such things. Whatever you have learned or received or heard from me, or seen in me—put it into practice. And the God of peace will be with you.

DAY 1 //worry

One morning before preschool, I was brushing my four-year-old daughter's hair after a shower. "You have beautiful hair like your birth mom," I told her. "I miss her!" she replied. "Do you know where she lives so you can take me to visit her?" she asked.

My four-year-old daughter doesn't remember much about her birth parents since she has lived with us from infancy, but she knows about her adoption. In the depths of her little heart, she has a special place reserved for her birth mom and dad, and I encourage that.

This peace I now have about the place of my child's birth parents did not come naturally. When she was a tiny baby, I was convinced that my daughter would not have a healthy attachment to me. She was difficult to soothe, resistant to sleep, and showed no fear of strangers. In my mind, these were signs of an attachment disorder caused by my failure to secure an early bond with her. My husband would try to reassure me that she was fine, but the fears still remained.

Despite these fears, I wanted my daughter to know how I treasure the beautiful things about her that come from her biological family. I intentionally looked for ways to *rejoice in the Lord* about my daughter's genetics. I have hazel eyes and my husband's eyes are bright blue, but she is our brown-eyed girl. We are both very tall, but she is so very tiny. We were both generally compliant children, and she is full of fire and strong will. I love all of these things about her so much. I want her to know this. I love all of her, even and especially the traits that don't come from how I am raising her.

In my heart, I know God chose her to be my daughter, just as Ephesians 1:5 says *he predestined us for adoption to sonship through Jesus Christ, in accordance with his pleasure and will.* His hand was always upon her, protecting her, keeping her safe for me. He prompted her birth mother's heart to pick up the phone at a desperate time and ask me to take her tiny precious baby into my home. He provided clothing and diapers and bottles and babysitters through people led by his Spirit to love us into our new role as parents. He calmed my anxious heart and answered my desperate prayers to make her forever mine.

I am the mother that he chose for my daughter, not because of my great wisdom, but because of my complete dependence upon his guidance. Because he is faithful, I am able to trust. And when I trust, I am somehow able to enjoy those potentially fearful moments with her rather than **worry** the days away.

*Lord, when **worry** starts to take over my mind, help me to find joy in parenting the child you have chosen for me.*

DAY 2 //worry

The mounting pressures of my career and the whirlwind speed at which our family was growing resulted in **worry** taking over in my mind. Life as an adoptive mom, social worker, and ministry wife triggered many relationship difficulties with my children and husband. In my anxious state of mind, I began barking orders to my children and my husband. The more overwhelmed I felt, the harsher my words and actions became.

One evening, we were rushing around to leave the house, running late as usual. My middle daughter was not picking up the pace despite my repeated orders to get in the SUV, and I completely lost my cool. I started screeching at her to "get in the car!" at the top of my lungs, flailing my arms around in exasperation. Tears welled up in her eyes as she climbed into the back seat. I shut the door and looked to my husband for sympathy, but that is not what I received.

Gently, ever so lovingly, my husband redirected my path. He placed his hands on my shoulders and helped me gain perspective. Yes, our daughter was being slow, but I had completely overreacted. I climbed into the passenger seat, spun around to see my daughter hanging her head in the back seat, and felt ashamed. I apologized for yelling at her and asked for forgiveness, which she quickly granted with a smile. We went on with our evening, and I felt a calm come over my spirit.

Since my natural response to stress is to lash out in anger, I must consciously choose to *let my gentleness be evident* to my children. The New Living Translation puts verse 5 (in Phil. 4) like this: *Let everyone see that you are considerate in all you do. Remember, the Lord is coming soon.*

I have to admit, I am not always considerate of my children's feelings. Because they have experienced abuse and neglect in their biological families, my kids are extra sensitive to any tone of disapproval or shame in my voice. I know I need to calm my emotions first so my children receive *my love* along with discipline, but sometimes I still fail in this area. I need to remember that the Lord is near. His peace is available to me when I feel anxious inside. His peace will calm my heart if I allow him to work in me.

Lord, help me keep my attitude in check, letting my gentleness be evident to all, remembering that connection with my children should precede correction.

DAY 3 *//worry*

From a very young age, my son Braydyn, has demonstrated faithfulness in prayer. One particular example of his absolute trust in the power of his prayers comes to mind. When Braydyn overheard me telling my husband about a high school football player who suffered a traumatic brain injury, he prayed for that young man to get back on the football field. He was persistent in prayer every night, and before the end of that football season, the injured player dressed in uniform and stood on the sidelines with his team. Braydyn was so excited to find out that God had answered his prayers!

In contrast, I tend to become very anxious in the midst of difficult circumstances, thinking of the worst possible outcome. Particularly when my children were in foster care, I felt powerless to protect them. After all, they were wards of the court, where a judge considered the reports from their caseworker, therapist, and guardian ad litem to determine their fate. Even after praying over my fears, my mind would race with thoughts of "what if...". *What if the caseworker recommends reunification? What if the therapist doesn't think our home is appropriate? What if the judge denies our petition for adoption? What if the court removes my daughter from my home?*

Rather than **worry**, God commands us not to fear. *Do not be anxious about anything, but in every situation, by prayer and petition, with thanksgiving, present your requests to God (verse 6 in Phil. 4).* Regardless of the circumstances, Christ wants us to trust him with the outcome. This does not mean that we should never have feelings of anxiety or thoughts of **worry**. Rather, when these feelings and thoughts come into our hearts and mind, we overcome them through prayer and petition to God. Once we present our requests, we must allow his peace to guard our hearts and minds from anxiety.

Although the risk about the future doesn't ever really go away, I have had to believe that God had the final say in their case, as well as in their lives. Proverbs 21:1 (NLT) says *"The king's heart is like a stream of water directed by the LORD; he guides it wherever he pleases."* I prayed this scripture over the judge, choosing to trust God for the outcome, knowing that he was in control.

Lord, take my anxious thoughts and help me trust you. I need your peace to guard my heart and mind.

DAY 4 //worry

Another **worry** battle I constantly fight in my mind is a tendency to dwell on the negative. I find myself replaying the failures of the past and fearing the worst for the future. This thought pattern is especially common when it comes to my thoughts about one particular child. She was sexually abused by her father, yet her mother chose to stay in the marriage even after the abuse was exposed.

As she has shared these difficult details with me, I have grieved over the depths of her pain from her parents' rejection and betrayal. I longed to fill in the gaping hole in her soul with my love, but it was never enough. I desperately want to fix her, to change her heart, to help her see the beauty that could come from brokenness. I worried that in her pain, she would shut out the world. But truthfully, I worried that she would shut *me* out.

The thought terrified me that one day soon she would graduate high school and never look back. Inside my mind, I allowed thoughts about negative circumstances to choke out the joy of all the good the Lord was accomplishing in my family.

As newly adoptive parents, my husband and I struggled not to ride the roller coaster of our daughter's emotional suffering. We experienced times of great connection with her followed by extended periods of detachment and rejection. In these difficult times, I battled my anxiety with prayer. I wept for her pain, begging for God to *repay the years the locusts have eaten* from her life (using a reference from Joel 2:25).

Soon after joining our family, this child began a relationship with Jesus Christ. I marveled at the change in her as she allowed the Holy Spirit to move in her life. Before Christ, she strongly identified with the lyrics of a suicidal and drug addicted musician. Now, she passionately sings "there is power in the name of Jesus to break every chain" as she strums her acoustic guitar.

Jesus knows the depths of depravity and evil that my daughter's biological parents exposed her to. He also knows I am incapable of healing her wounds, yet he entrusted her life into my hands anyway. I must choose to trust the One who will repay the years the locusts have eaten from her life, the years of abuse, neglect, abandonment, and shame.

When **worry** starts to fill my heart, I must be intentional about my thoughts. Philippians 4:8 instructs that *whatever is true, whatever is noble, whatever is right, whatever is pure, whatever is lovely, whatever is admirable—if anything is excellent or praiseworthy—think about such things.* God does not command me to do the impossible. With the help of the Holy Spirit, I can *take every my thoughts captive to make it obedient to Christ.*

Lord, take away my anxious thoughts and replace them with thoughts of that are true, noble, pure, lovely, admirable, excellent, and praiseworthy.

DAY 5 //worry

As I have transitioned into parenting an adult child, I must *put into practice what I have learned* over the years even more, trusting that *the God of peace will be with me*. Some of the fears and **worries** that plagued my mind about attachment, rejection, and long-term effects of abuse and neglect have come true. As my oldest child graduated high school and moved out on her own, our relationship has challenged me more than ever before.

In order to feel safe, she needs to feel in control of her relationship with me. Now that she is an adult, we sometimes go months without speaking. Milestones that I expected would be joyful: like her wedding day or when she gave birth to her daughter, often trigger a separation between us. When she draws near again, I treasure the connection, but I have come to expect her to pull away again.

Naturally, this is deeply painful to me as her mother. I want to share in these precious times, hold her hand, pray with her, and celebrate the miracles God has done in her life. But she doesn't need me in the same way that my other children need a mom. She values our relationship, but there will always be a difference in the way we connect. I came into her life at a crucial time of adolescence, after much of her personality and perspective had already developed. I cannot pretend to have more influence over her than I truly do. She loves me. She respects me. I am her family, but in her heart, I am not her mother.

At least not in the same way that in my heart, she is my daughter.

This is where the true practice of peace becomes a daily reality for me. I have peace that it is not my place to fix my children, and that my worth as a person does not depend on how they feel about me. Even if my children all reject me, I will still have love in my most important relationship with Jesus Christ. And that is my ultimate prayer for my children, that they will have a relationship with Jesus Christ as well. In the end, for eternity, we will all be in perfect peace with him.

Lord, even more than I want my daughter to love me, I want her to know the love of you, her heavenly Father. Thank you for your relentless love of her.

beholding Christ

This week we focus on the topic of *beholding* Christ in adoption and parenting. **JULIE SWAIN** uses 2 Corinthians 4:6-18 to remind us of our privilege to *behold*—that is, *to gaze at, contemplate,* or *observe*—Christ in the midst of unknown and difficult circumstances.

As Julie explains, there is great temptation within every parent to see themselves and their circumstances in such a way that removes our focus from Jesus. The Gospel work that God longs to do in the lives of adoptive families involves beholding the work of Christ, done on our behalf, that we were helpless and hopeless to do for ourselves. In this *beholding of him* is where freedom is found to rest in his completed work, no matter how incomplete our work or unknown the circumstances around us may be. As we behold ourselves and our circumstances less and less, we **behold Christ** more and more.

SCRIPTURE FOCUS //2 CORINTHIANS 4:6-18 (ESV)

For God, who said, "Let light shine out of darkness," has shone in our hearts to give the light of the knowledge of the glory of God in the face of Jesus Christ.

But we have this treasure in jars of clay, to show that the surpassing power belongs to God and not to us. We are afflicted in every way, but not crushed; perplexed, but not driven to despair; persecuted, but not forsaken; struck down, but not destroyed; always carrying in the body the death of Jesus, so that the life of Jesus may also be manifested in our bodies. For we who live are always being given over to death for Jesus' sake, so that the life of Jesus also may be manifested in our mortal flesh. So death is at work in us, but life in you.

Since we have the same spirit of faith according to what has been written, "I believed, and so I spoke," we also believe, and so we also speak, knowing that he who raised the Lord Jesus will raise us also with Jesus and bring us with you into his presence. For it is all for your sake, so that as grace extends to more and more people it may increase thanksgiving, to the glory of God.

So we do not lose heart. Though our outer self is wasting away, our inner self is being renewed day by day. For this light momentary affliction is preparing for us an eternal weight of glory beyond all comparison, as we look not to the things that are seen but to the things that are unseen. For the things that are seen are transient, but the things that are unseen are eternal.

DAY 1 *Beholding Christ*

For God, who said, "Let light shine out of darkness," has shone in our hearts to give the light of the knowledge of the glory of God in the face of Jesus Christ.
—2 Corinthians 4:6 (ESV)

It can be overwhelming to consider the degree of darkness that many orphans have endured while waiting for their forever families. We received pictures of our daughter from a camera we had sent the orphanage shortly after receiving our approval, and we were disheartened to see that every indoor picture was in darkness.

Imagine spending the first years of your life in utter physical darkness.

We would most likely become accustomed to it... and possibly even grow to prefer it. CJ Mahaney, pastor at Sovereign Grace Church in Louisville, Kentucky, shared in a sermon more about these realities of adoption. He spoke about a family who had adopted two boys out of an orphanage in Russia. The conditions there were horrid. They were not fed regularly. They only got diaper changes once or twice a day, and they received minimal care overall. Yet when their new parents drove away, the kids were screaming in terror and reaching back for the orphanage.

When I read the book of Exodus, I used to get puzzled by how the Israelites longed to go back to Egypt after they had been set free. Now I understand better... they were just released from bondage and slavery, *but the unknown future was more frightening than their known past.*

I know that I tend to be the child screaming in terror and reaching back towards a squalid orphanage because I don't always trust the love of my Father who seeks to take me away to something better. Change can be really scary. But when Jesus changes our hearts, he doesn't just change a few things.

He changes everything.

God spoke and said, *"Let light shine out of darkness..."* He gives us eyes to see Christ... to **behold** him for who he is. And when that happens, our perspective and focus changes completely. No longer will our view merely be the dark walls of an orphanage and its earthly circumstances. Instead, in **beholding** Christ, we can find hope in the glory of God.

*Lord, we praise you for pulling us out of darkness. May we **behold** your glory in the face of Jesus Christ more and more, while **beholding** what life once was as orphans less and less. Thank you, Jesus, for having a plan all along to rescue and redeem us into our forever family.*

DAY 2 *Beholding Christ*

But we have this treasure in jars of clay, to show that the surpassing power belongs to God and not to us. We are afflicted in every way, but not crushed; perplexed, but not driven to despair; persecuted, but not forsaken; struck down, but not destroyed; always carrying in the body the death of Jesus, so that the life of Jesus may also be manifested in our bodies. —2 Corinthians 4:7-10 (ESV)

I think that within every mother is a tendency to behold, or focus on, our martyrdom. Sometimes the afflicting, perplexing, persecuting, and struck down realities that come with motherhood can become all-consuming. Before one Cheerio even hits the floor, I can find myself predicting how many I will sweep up in a given day. And the list of labors is endless; it always is.

But there is so much more for us in motherhood than just recounting the list. There's a greater focus than the one that gets through the day repeating, "I am laying down my life for Christ." The calling of parenting through adoption is about more than our service, our works, our feats for our children... it is about so much more than us laying our lives down. Are we truly created to behold our tribulations with every hurdle and setback along the way? In doing so, are we **beholding** the Gospel as God intended?

In the midst of the list, there is Good News, and more to **behold**. While being a mom is hard work, there is One who came to this earth and did *the ultimate work*. We are merely the limited and weak jars of clay, and yet we carry this treasure to show that the surpassing power to love our children belongs to God and not to us. We will be afflicted, perplexed, persecuted, and struck down; in him we are not crushed, driven to despair, forsaken, or destroyed.

He came to do for us what we could never do for ourselves. He lived a life of humbly serving and loving his enemies. He died a death that he did not deserve to bring us into his grace... he is and has always been in the business of redeeming his beloved church. *We are his.*

And I believe that freedom in Christ in any area, but especially in how it relates to motherhood, is found in **beholding** this incredible Savior again, and again, and again. Instead of how hard we are working to keep our homes and families in running order, let us contemplate THE work done that allowed our hearts to change and be in "running order" in the first place. Instead of exalting the service we do in laying our lives down for our children, let us exalt THE One who was the perfect example of a servant in laying his life down. In beholding the One who has adopted us into his forever family, we are *"always carrying in the body the death of Jesus, so that the life of Jesus may also be manifested in our bodies."*

*Lord, fix our eyes upon you. May we **behold** the work of Christ more and more, and behold ourselves less and less.*

DAY 3 *Beholding Christ*

For we who live are always being given over to death for Jesus' sake, so that the life of Jesus also may be manifested in our mortal flesh. So death is at work in us, but life in you. Since we have the same spirit of faith according to what has been written, "I believed, and so I spoke," we also believe, and so we also speak, knowing that he who raised the Lord Jesus will raise us also with Jesus and bring us with you into his presence. For it is all for your sake, so that as grace extends to more and more people it may increase thanksgiving, to the glory of God. —2 Corinthians 4:11-15 (ESV)

For God to adopt us as his children, a death had to happen. Christ was punished and crucified for our sin. He died on a cross, paying our ransom. The Gospel call is not only "come and live," but it is "come and die... so that you may live." The only way for the life of Jesus to be manifested in our mortal flesh is for us to be given over to death for Jesus' sake. We must die to our tendency towards self, to turn from sin and towards Christ. As in the Gospel work that has taken place in our hearts through Christ, a death must also happen in the journey of adoption. Not merely the death of a dream, as birth families relinquish their precious blood-born kin. But many, many deaths must happen, within the hearts of adoptive parents, to experience the redemption God has planned for the little ones he entrusts into our care.

There are difficult days when I begin to resent the cup given to me... when the "deaths" of sin seem unbearable even with an overflowing serving of grace, especially in the area of bonding and attaching to my daughter. Many days it feels like we are still an ocean apart even when we are sitting at the same kitchen table. I've come to realize that much of the distance between us is a result of my own self-protective heart, although I was not expecting that to be the case. I'm learning to die, perhaps daily, to walls, guards, and self-protection in this attachment dance.

My husband spoke into my life on such a day when he said, "You want the resurrection without the cross." *Ouch.* But God promised us that, "*he who raised the Lord Jesus will raise us also with Jesus and bring us into his presence.*" God has written the story from beginning to end... he already knows how he is going to redeem the broken lives in our homes. He is the Author, the One who sees the final resurrection of those who have died in Christ... he who began a good work in us has promised to complete the work.

"*For it is all for your sake, so that as grace extends to more and more people it may increase thanksgiving, to the glory of God.*" May we thank God for the grace he extends to us "to come and die so that we may live." May we **behold** Christ, so he always receive the glory for the cross and resurrection that happens daily in our homes.

Lord, thank you that while given over to death for Jesus' sake, we also are given eternal life in him. We know that you will raise us up with Christ and bring us into your presence for eternity.

DAY 4 *Beholding Christ*

So we do not lose heart. Though our outer self is wasting away, our inner self is being renewed day by day. —2 Corinthians 4:16 (ESV)

I know that there is something deeply broken within me. My outer self is wasting away. Who will enter into my brokenness? *Jesus will.* His uninhibited grace renews my inner self day by day. It enters into the darkness and bears light. It brings forth a response of falling to my knees before a holy yet loving God. It always initiates. It is always available. It never avoids. Grace has taught me who I want to be through Christ, and who I already am in Christ. There is always more room at the foot of the cross, as together we **behold** our Christ.

Sometimes the growing pains of raising a child from hard places remind me of this beautifully messy truth. I often limp through these "day by days" barely hanging onto this grace in mothering our precious daughter due to my own brokenness. Our daughter has brokenness within her too. I am sure there are days that she wonders if anyone wants to enter into her pain. She will one day long for a Love that will go the distance for her when it seems like all earthly love has failed her. We will point her to the One Who will. He moved heaven and earth to be with her, to carry her burdens, and to heal her heart. I pray that this precious grace would come through Christ into her brokenness, to redeem and heal what is broken as he has been so faithful to do in mine. *No brokenness is ever wasted.*

In moments like these, that take me back to the cross, I recall a Puritan prayer entitled *The Valley of Vision*. It reminds me that his way for me is not the easiest way, but it is the only path that leads to true healing and lasting change in beholding Christ. It is the valley of vision.

Lord, high and holy, meek and lowly,
Thou hast brought me to the valley of vision,
Where I live in the depths but see Thee in the heights;
Hemmed in by mountains of sin
I behold Thy glory.
Let me learn by paradox
That the way down is the way up,
That to be low is to be high,
That the broken heart is the healed heart,
That the contrite spirit is the rejoicing spirit,
That the repenting soul is the victorious soul,
That to have nothing is to possess all,
That to bear the cross is to wear the crown,
That to give is to receive,
That the valley is the place of vision.
Lord, in the daytime stars can be seen from deepest wells,
And the deeper the wells the brighter thy stars shine;

Let me find thy light in my darkness,
Thy life in my death,
Thy joy in my sorrow,
Thy grace in my sin,
Thy riches in my poverty,
Thy glory in my valley.

Lord, we praise you that although our outer self is wasting away, that no brokenness is wasted. Thank you for renewing us day by day, and for writing the story of redemption upon our hearts.

DAY 5 *Beholding Christ*

For this light momentary affliction is preparing for us an eternal weight of glory beyond all comparison, as we look not to the things that are seen but to the things that are unseen. For the things that are seen are transient, but the things that are unseen are eternal. —2 Corinthians 4:17-18 (ESV)

During our time in China, we visited one of the world's greatest historic landmarks... the Great Wall. We had heard a lot of people describe how hard the climb was, but we have to admit that we underestimated it.

Something we learned right away is that the Great Wall cannot be climbed in view of every step that is ahead. The summit is designed for one to only see one section of the wall at a time. If we were to see all the steps ahead of us to reach the top, most of us would not even attempt such a task.

God used this aspect of climbing the Great Wall to remind us of the gift of beholding Christ through adoption. In the journey of adoption, we have found that there will be momentary affliction. There will be brokenness in need of the redemptive work of Jesus Christ. And yet, if we were to see all of the steps that we need to climb to scale the wall of our children's hearts... we would probably turn and run. Such a feat would be impossible without a focus on the unseen eternal in Christ.

As in the Great Wall, God gives us the measure of grace required to climb just the next step in front of us in adoption. The climb is accomplished when one trusts in what is unseen to carry them through what is seen. In the midst of momentary affliction, God has promised us that he is preparing for us an eternal weight of glory beyond all comparison.

As we climbed the Great Wall, we were literally on our hands and knees at some points, barely able to catch our breath in the thick of high altitude. And that is how it has been in this process of adopting our daughter. There are days when we are on our hands and knees crying out to God for answers and the strength to fight for her heart.

Through climbing the Great Wall of China, we sensed God inviting us to fix our eyes on Christ to climb each and every step that was before us. We rest in knowing that we can climb any mountain that he lays before us through focusing on his Son who climbed the mountain to our hearts on Calvary. He reminds us daily that he has equipped us to take each step in his grace, by **beholding** Christ's face *"as we look not to the things that are seen but to the things that are unseen."* We rest in knowing that although we do not see every step to reach the unseen, that he has written the story of redemption purposefully for our good and his glory.

Lord, even when the climb is filled with unknowns, may we fix our eyes on you to take each step before us. In your care, we can climb the wall of our children's hearts as you have done for us.

fear

Fear of the unknown is a common barrier for most of us. So often when facing trials, we become immobilized by the **fear** of what we cannot see, and what we cannot control. Adoption, for most of us, is characterized *the unknown*. So how do we approach it with peace? This week, adoptive mom **TONJA IHLENFELDT** offers insight on doing just that—and four practical steps we can all take to remove **fear** from our lives—from Paul's letter to the people of Philippi.

SCRIPTURE FOCUS //PHILIPPIANS 4:4-9 (NKJV)

Rejoice in the Lord always. Again I will say, rejoice! Let your gentleness be known to all men. The Lord is at hand.

Be anxious for nothing, but in everything by prayer and supplication, with thanksgiving, let your requests be made known to God; and the peace of God, which surpasses all understanding, will guard your hearts and minds through Christ Jesus.

Finally, brethren, whatever things are true, whatever things are noble, whatever things are just, whatever things are pure, whatever things are lovely, whatever things are of good report, if there is any virtue and if there is anything praiseworthy—meditate on these things. The things which you learned and received and heard and saw in me, these do, and the God of peace will be with you.

DAY 1 //fear

In recent years, we found ourselves surrounded by friends who adopted. While we whole-heartedly supported their ventures, we never dreamed we would add more children to our already large family. However, God dropped into our hearts a boy who needed us.

After months of searching, mounds of paperwork, and tons of money, we left to adopt a brother (and his sister!) in Nicaragua, with neither a photo nor any sort of biographical information about the kids. What we did have was a God-given promise that this was his will for us. The greatest stretch of my faith, during our four months in Central America, was to *not* let **fear** take over in my life.

Living in a foreign country, away from all of our family and friends, while fostering two older children, is a formula that equals **fear**. All of the preliminary planning and excitement of following God's plan to adopt did not prepare me for the **fear** I would deal with during our fostering period. Within the first few days we experienced earthquakes, a car accident, extreme heat, lack of housing, and an inability to communicate with our adoption attorney. **Fear** quickly began to try to make it's home in my mind. I needed answers, and fast. So I asked God for help. Philippians 4 is what he used to pull me out of the "snare of **fear**" that threatened to overwhelm me.

Rejoice in the Lord always. Again I will say, rejoice! Let your gentleness be known to all men. The Lord is at hand. Be anxious for nothing, but in everything by prayer and supplication, with thanksgiving, let your requests be made known to God; and the peace of God, which surpasses all understanding, will guard your hearts and minds through Christ Jesus. Finally, brethren, whatever things are true, whatever things are noble, whatever things are just, whatever things are pure, whatever things are lovely, whatever things are of good report, if there is any virtue and if there is anything praiseworthy—meditate on these things. —Philippians 4:4-8

With this passage, God showed me four clear steps that I began to use as a formula to avoid **fear**. After all, God tells us in Isaiah 41:10 (ESV) to "***Fear*** *not, for I am with you.*" If God says not to be afraid there has to be a way to get rid of it!

Step 1: *Rejoice in the Lord.*

First, remind yourself daily of the promises of God, with scripture that says how good he is and what he as already done for you. Say these out loud in prayer to God. This will build and strengthen your faith. It will get you to *see* correctly and not focus on your problem. (Remember, Peter had faith to walk on the water *until* he began to focus on the waves!)

Thank you, Father, that all things work together for good to those who love you. (Romans 8:28) Thank you for always causing me to triumph in Christ Jesus! (2 Cor. 2:14)

DAY 2 //fear

Being afraid is something God actually commands us *not* to do. The problem is we all have circumstances that thrust **fear** before our face, and inject it into the very fabric of our lives. We have fooled ourselves into thinking it's ok to live with **fear** while still believing God. **Fear** is sly like that. **Fear** can disguise itself as worry, anxiety, or simply being unable to think about anything other than the problem at hand.

That's what happened to me.

I found myself in Nicaragua, with everything around me unsure and nothing that made any sense. I couldn't sleep and I couldn't eat, as the physical effects of fear took over my body. I was preoccupied with worry about how long I would be in country, and anxiety about my husband and children that were living without me back home. *Was I damaging my family? Would this foreign country be safe?*

When each of these circumstances began to overwhelm me, I had to purposefully go to God every time, with each of the steps to combat **fear**.

Step 1: *Rejoice in the Lord.*

Step 2: *Be anxious for nothing, but in everything by prayer and supplication, with thanksgiving, let your requests be made known to God.*

Prayer involves talking and listening, connecting and responding. In order to facilitate this process of eliminating fear, we need to work it all out in a daily communion with God. First John 4:18 (NKJV) tells us, *"There is no **fear** in love; but perfect love casts out **fear** because **fear** involves torment. But he who **fears** is not made perfect in love."*

Did you catch that? *There is no **fear** in love!* Perfect love (which can only be found in God) actually casts out **fear**!

Drawing close to God, and reminding ourselves how much he loves us, eliminates **fear** and gives us answers. We must fight to spend the time with him. When we're in the midst of it, we won't feel like praying, because we have too much to worry about! David spent time singing to God while watching sheep in the pasture lands. He found a way to incorporate communion with God into even the mundane aspects of his day. And that relationship resulted in a believer who ran at Goliath, unafraid and fully convinced God would defeat his enemy with a stone.

Father God, I don't want to live in fear! I love you, and trust you to walk one step ahead of me to cast out all fear before it ensnares me.

DAY 3 //fear

As I began everyday reminding myself of God's promises and praying, I found myself calm and better able to deal with situations as they came. I remember one particular day, during our fostering period, when I received some devastating news. In Nicaragua, the consejo—or council—meets once every month or so to approve pending adoption cases. Your case must be on the docket before the council actually meets in order for your case to be heard.

Our attorney told us that we would make the consejo for the month of May without a problem. So my husband flew in to help bring us home. Imagine our shock when the council met and we discovered our case had *not*, in fact, been heard. For two months I had been telling myself, "I can do this; we'll be home by the second week in June!" Yet here I stood, understanding it would be another four to six weeks before the next consejo meeting, and then another two to three weeks to wrap things up before we could be home.

I felt tears well up in my eyes as I realized my husband had to leave and I would be in Nicaragua for perhaps another two months. I cried for a short time, while my husband held me, and then I was done.

Peace was there.

I knew everything was going to be all right. Did my situation change? *No.* Did I have peace? *Yes!*

Step 1: *Rejoice in the Lord.*

Step 2: *Be anxious for nothing, but in everything by prayer and supplication, with thanksgiving, let your requests be made known to God.*

Step 3: *...and the peace of God, which surpasses all understanding, will guard your hearts and minds through Christ Jesus.*

Peace is different in the kingdom of God than what the world teaches. God's peace, the peace that Jesus said he gives to us according to John, in Chapter 14, is a peace that we have in the midst of a storm. Our situation may not change, but we have peace. Jesus slept through a storm, then at the request of his frightened disciples, he spoke to the storm and it became still.

Many times during our stay in Nicaragua, I should have been "freaking out" but somehow I wasn't. I recall one day I found myself with my 20-year-old daughter and our two new children walking along a dangerous road unable to find a cab to drive us home. Local people were staring at us and I knew this was not the place for us to be walking alone. *But peace was with us.* I did not give in to **fear** or panic. I asked God for help as I calmly, yet quickly hustled the children onward, until eventually a cab came.

Lord, thank you that when we rejoice in you, bringing you all of our needs in prayer and thanksgiving, you guard our hearts and minds with your glorious peace.

DAY 4 //fear

As you begin to rejoice in the Lord, give your cares to him and experience his peace, your mind will begin to fight with you. Thoughts come at you, often like a machine gun, trying to force you back into **fear**, trying to force you to leave the promises of God. This is why the passage in Philippians warns us to think about good things.

Finally, brethren, whatever things are true, whatever things are noble, whatever things are just, whatever things are pure, whatever things are lovely, whatever things are of good report, if there is any virtue and if there is anything praiseworthy — meditate on these things. The things which you learned and received and heard and saw in me, these do, and the God of peace will be with you. (Philippians 4:8-9 NKJV)

How do I stop myself from thinking on the bad things, the bad report? I can hear you now saying, "I can't help what I think about!" If the bible tells us that we can, *we can!* Everyone needs to discover what it takes to stop her own mind. Here are some ways I discovered I could control my thoughts.

First, make yourself talk about the promise of God. Tell your kids what God has promised. Tell a friend. *You can't think about something different than what you are talking about.*

Second, ignore people who want to tell you "worst case scenarios" or their terrible experiences that resulted in terrible results. Yes we need to beware of dangers around us, and not be blind to situations that can harm us, but when we are fighting fear, our enemy will "conveniently" surround us with people who enjoy telling their *war stories* without talking about how they were able to overcome. *Christ always overcomes!*

Finally, do something for someone else. This will get your mind off of yourself and your problem. I found if I kept myself busy, I could distract my thoughts.

Our focus always needs to be on the promises of God. Joseph had a dream that God gave to him. God did not tell Joseph his brothers would betray him and he would end up in prison before his dream would come to pass. *But God gave Joseph that promise to focus on.*

When things get tough, when situations seem to delay our dream, we must focus on the promise. Do not allow yourself to dive into the fear. Stay in faith and do not quit.

Father God, you know my fears. You know my worst case scenarios. Help me focus instead of your promises and that you have already won!

DAY 5 //fear

The kids and I watched a movie called *After Earth* where the alien enemy could only find the humans if they displayed **fear**. If the soldier's heart rate began to increase or if the soldier began to exhibit panic in some way, they were told to "take a knee." One commander told a young soldier that "danger is real but **fear** is a choice." This is so true in the Kingdom of God. If we can "take a knee" and allow our Heavenly Father to strengthen our heart, and to remind ourselves of how good our God is, we will have peace in the midst of a storm. We will be able endure until the promise comes to pass.

Hebrews 4 tells us the Israelites were unable to enter the Promised Land because of unbelief. We have to labor to enter into his rest. Everything around us will scream that the promise of God can't happen. *It's impossible.* But remember, with God, *all things are possible!*

Step 1: *Rejoice in the Lord.*

Step 2: *Be anxious for nothing, but in everything by prayer and supplication, with thanksgiving, let your requests be made known to God.*

Step 3: *...and the peace of God, which surpasses all understanding, will guard your hearts and minds through Christ Jesus.*

Step 4: *Finally, brethren, whatever things are true, whatever things are noble, whatever things are just, whatever things are pure, whatever things are lovely, whatever things are of good report, if there is any virtue and if there is anything praiseworthy —meditate on these things. The things which you learned and received and heard and saw in me, these do, and the God of peace will be with you.*

We endured four months of constant temptation to **fear** while living in Nicaragua. I am pleased to tell you we made it through. Looking back on our time in country, I am thankful for the lessons God taught me about staying in faith and not giving into **fear**. I have personally battled **fear** my whole life and I can honestly say that my experiences during our adoption process have drawn me closer to God and enabled me to face most any situation without **fear**.

When we arrived back in the U.S., my perspective on life had dramatically changed. Situations that previously felt overwhelming seem small to me now. I feel like David must have when he ran at Goliath. He had first seen God defeat the lion and the bear using David's own limited strength and ability. So when David later came face to face with the giant, what came out if his mouth was complete confidence in his God. This is how I want to face life: *feed my faith and leave **fear** far behind!*

Not only did God prevail in our adoption as we now have two wonderful additions to our family, he brought us home safe, provided all of our needs along the way, and caused us to overcome the midst of many storms.

Thank you Jesus! Thank you!

trust

This week's series focuses on a key lesson **JESSIE CRABTREE** and her husband learned during their adoption of Yader, in the country of Nicaragua. Throughout their fostering and adoption process, they—like most of us—faced many trials and much frustration over a process that never quite seemed to go as planned. As Jessie shares, she just had to hold on to the fact that no matter what, she could **trust** God to do what is best for her family.

PRIMARY SCRIPTURE FOCUS //LUKE 11:9-13 (NKJ)

"So I say to you, ask, and it will be given to you; seek, and you will find; knock, and it will be opened to you. For everyone who asks receives, and he who seeks finds, and to him who knocks it will be opened. If a son asks for bread from any father among you, will he give him a stone? Or if he asks for a fish, will he give him a serpent instead of a fish? Or if he asks for an egg, will he offer him a scorpion? If you then, being evil, know how to give good gifts to your children, how much more will your heavenly Father give the Holy Spirit to those who ask him!"

Note from Jessie: As a supplement to this week's devotional, I encourage you to prayerfully read over John 14-16 throughout the week. These chapters give comforting words of Jesus which pour over us the love and instruction that he has over us during uncertain times.

DAY 1 //trust

I remember when we first began praying that the Lord would give Yader to us as our son. It was almost too surreal to even verbalize a prayer! Such a wild possibility—that God would grant us the desire of our heart. But we began to pray, though vaguely at first: "Lord, if it is your will, please show us if we should really pursue adoption." It was difficult, in the beginning, to express our heart's desire to God.

While a sense of hopeful excitement encircled these prayers for our son, there was still this temptation to feel guilty to bring this before God. All of these anxious thoughts flew through my heart and mind, threatening to crowd out the hope: "He doesn't want me to be a beggar... Should I be asking God for something so beautiful? I don't deserve this... This would be too good to actually be true."

God's Word is powerful.

What a gift it is to be able to search the Word and learn profound, simple truths that touch us right where we are in life. Luke 11:9 presents a wonderful command and promise: "*So I say to you, ask, and it will be given to you; seek, and you will find; knock, and it will be opened to you.*"

In this passage, Jesus clearly gives three commands: Ask, seek, knock. Can you believe he actually needed to *command* us to do these things? They seem so simple, yet obviously we do *need* to hear this from Jesus, or it wouldn't be in the Bible. Another way to word these three commands is to verbalize to him, watch for him, and be proactive in bringing a desire or need to Jesus' feet.

Note that the verse is in present tense, meaning it touches even today's needs and desires! The passage also doesn't give an end to asking, seeking, and knocking. So, keep it up!

The great thing about these commands is that they invite us *to be specific*. Following them will likely require steps of faith into an unknown future. But aren't taking steps of faith where God's blessing lies?

If you abide in Me, and My words abide in you, you will ask what you desire, and it shall be done for you. —John 15:7

God repeatedly commands us to ask him for help. I suppose the question is this: do we **trust** him enough to meet them?

Lord, help me to have the faith to continually ask you to meet my needs and my heart's desires.

DAY 2 //trust

And so we continued praying and asking God for Yader. During the highs and lows of the adoption process, we continued to pray, "Lord, please give us to Yader, and give him to us! Your Word is clear that your heart is to bring the fatherless into families. Please join us together."

Then we became more specific and fervent, "Please grant this desire of our heart and give us Yader as our son. Let your Spirit lead us and let your will prevail. May the Devil flee from before us. Let me and my husband be unified and at peace. Rule my heart. Rule my husband's heart. Please do miracles. Be our advocate. Your will be done, Lord; your Kingdom come. "

For everyone who asks receives, and he who seeks finds, and to him who knocks it will be opened. Luke 11:10

What a promise: *"Everyone who asks…"* I think that oftentimes we pray half-heartedly. We ask God for something, without actually **trusting** him to answer. We need this promise in Scripture as well as the command to ask.

It's interesting to note that Scripture doesn't say you'll necessarily "receive what you ask for." When I let that thought enter into possibility, I was headed down a rabbit trail of what-ifs. What if God says no? What if he sends us in another direction? What will happen to Yader?

And then those what-ifs led to a bunch of it-will-never-happens.

Was God speaking to us through those negative voices and circum-stances we kept hearing? Was that our answer? Was our adoption of Yader impossible? I couldn't even bare the thought of it. Such a future felt utterly hopeless.

"…he who seeks finds…"

God doesn't want us to get caught up in what-ifs and it-will-never-happens. He wants us to love him and ask for the desires he places in our hearts. He wants us to seek him and his ways, and then **trust** him to provide.

So I force myself into a course correction: "Let Satan be bound in Jesus' Name! I don't want to live at the devil's whim. I'm miserable and feeling pretty worthless right now. Whose side am I on? This month ushers in the Thanksgiving season, but my thoughts show there is little I'm choosing to be thankful for."

Lord, today my specific request to you is _____. Please help an unbelief I have in my heart. Thank you for _____.

DAY 3 //trust

Yesterday we talked about praying specific prayers to ask God for the desires of our heart. While it didn't initially come easy, I got better at praying purposefully as our process continued. But then I still worried that God's answer might be less than what I was asking.

What if his answer would cause me to sink into an even deeper pit of depression with even less of a light at the end of the tunnel?

What if we don't get Yader?

What if we never have children?

What if we spend this Christmas without our family?

Some days, I found that my worry could quickly spiral away into the abyss of despair. I would get so caught up in the impossible, that I had no way to see the possible. God's Word has an answer for that. Better yet, he has a promise we can hold onto when we approach him in prayer.

Luke 11:11-12 tells us, *"If a son asks for bread from any father among you, will he give him a stone? Or if he asks for a fish, will he give him a serpent instead of a fish? Or if he asks for an egg, will he offer him a scorpion?"*

This Scripture passage is asking the question: Is God going to give a good gift? What if he gives a gift I don't want? Doesn't he know what I'm asking for is in line with what has been spelled out in Scripture? As we were waiting for Yader, I remember telling God, "Lord, hold me. Help me. Protect me. Lead me. *What are you doing here?* I'm worrying myself sick. I need you."

Think about it. What are the answers to these questions? What is the loving intent of any father in regard to meeting the desire and need of his child? Of course we know the answer is that he always has the best intentions!

Yes, but... what if? What if his answer is my worst-case-scenario? It all comes down to **trust**. Can I trust him? Do I trust my Father not to give me a stone when I ask for bread? Or, can I trust him even if his choice of bread is different than mine...

Perhaps the answer is in focusing not on *what if*, but *even if*.

*Lord, are you good? Can I **trust** you? Please show me your Hand in these circumstances.*

DAY 4 //trust

Toward the end of our journey waiting for Yader, I'd almost lost all hope. Due to the emotional highs and lows of the waiting period, as well as the uncertain answers we were hearing from family services, I'd fallen into a deep depression. As if to add insult to injury, I found myself at my lowest point right at the start of Thanksgiving in 2012. The thought of spending the holidays without the child I was yearning for left me feeling frustrated and bitter.

Our Christian fellowship group in Nicaragua, which was mostly comprised of missionaries from all over the States and other countries, held a special Thanksgiving service and meal. During that event they offered a time for participants to speak about what they were grateful for. I sat there listening to one person after another and quickly realized that I had little I wanted to be thankful for. I proceeded to silently tell God about my disappointment in him.

"If you then, being evil, know how to give good gifts to your children, how much more will your heavenly Father give the Holy Spirit to those who ask him!" —Luke 11:13

A parent knows to give good things to his child, right? Even when the child doesn't know how to ask? And even when the child doesn't know how to be grateful? Of course! We love our children and want to give them good gifts to bring joy and happiness.

Yet, even on our best day as parents, *God is greater.*

So, if we **trust** him to be our heavenly Father, we can **trust** him with to provide... even when we don't know how to ask and even when we aren't grateful. He sees past our failures to give us our daily provision and the desires he places in our hearts. *He is greater.*

"And whatever you ask in My name, that I will do, that the Father may be glorified in the Son. If you ask anything in My name, I will do it." —John 14:13-14

When I stopped to consider all of the amazing promises held in these passages, my anticipation that God would soon clearly answer was heightened more than ever before.

We can **trust** him to answer!

Lord, forgive my ungratefulness! I know you love me and want to give good gifts to me, your child. I **trust** *you to see these circumstances through! Thank you in advance for your answer!*

DAY 5 //trust

Just as I told God of my ungrateful heart during the sharing time at the missionary fellowship meal, he just as quickly reminded me of Luke 11:9-13. So after a few minutes, in my humility, I stood up and shared with the fellowship what my heart was sincerely saying, and what God was clearly reminding me.

*"And I tell you, **ask, and it will be given to you**; seek, and you will find; knock, and it will be opened to you. For **everyone who asks receives**, and the one who seeks finds, and to the one who knocks it will be opened. What father among you, if his son asks for a fish, will instead of a fish give him a serpent; or if he asks for an egg, will give him a scorpion? If you then, who are evil, know how to give good gifts to your children, **how much more will** the heavenly Father give the Holy Spirit to those who ask him!"* —Luke 11:9-13

The timing of this was amazing... God answered our prayer, but he chose when. Less than two weeks after Thanksgiving, we were completely surprised to find out that we would begin the foster-to-adopt period! What a moment filled with pure joy in realizing that God heard the prayer of our hearts and gave us what we asked for, and so much more!

"Now to him who is able to do exceedingly abundantly above all that we ask or think, according to the power that works in us, to him be glory in the church by Christ Jesus to all generations, forever and ever. Amen." —Ephesians 3:20-21

Note that the passage we've been reading in Luke invites us to make *specific* requests to God. In the same way, I believe that God is ready to give *specific* answers to those requests, if only we will **trust** him to do good through them. Remember that the way God responds truly is his answer to that request, and not just some happenstance.

As we end this week's devotional on **trusting** God, here are a few words of encouragement and suggestions:

» Be intentional in asking and watch in expectancy for the Lord's answer to your request.

» God may or may not allow you to see the end result, just as Moses and Jeremiah didn't see the end result in their lifetime. Note that the passage in Luke does not give a timeline to God answering. His answer could be quick, or it could come in years or generations. Leave this up to him.

» Remember that *God will answer!*

» Replace your *what-ifs* with *even-ifs*.

» Expect good things to come.

"Ask, and you will receive, that your joy may be full." —John 16:24

Oh, Lord! Hear the needs of my life and the desires of my heart! I trust you to hear and answer!

joy

"The Joy of the Lord is my strength," right? *So why am I unhappy?!* Christians have long discussed the difference between happiness (temporal) and joy (eternal). So, it seems appropriate to include a week for us to talk about **joy** in adoption.

Each adoption story is unique, but every single one has trials and challenges. As this week's author, **LAURA PHENEGER**, shares, those trials can threaten to steal our **joy** and perhaps even derail the adoption altogether. Laura reminds us that **joy** has nothing to do with our circumstances, and everything to do with our attitude.

SCRIPTURE FOCUS

Rejoice in The Lord always. I will say it again: Rejoice!...The Lord is near. —Phil. 4:4 & 5b (NIV)

Consider it pure joy pure joy, my brothers and sisters, whenever you face trials of many kinds, because you know that the testing of your faith produces perseverance. —James 1:2-3 (NIV)

You make known to me the path of life; you will fill me with joy in your presence, with eternal pleasures at your right hand. —Psalm 16:11 (NIV)

Clap your hands, all you nations; shout to God with cries of joy. How awesome is The Lord Most High, the great King over all the earth. He subdued nations under us, peoples under our feet. —Psalm 47:1-3 (NIV)

For you make me glad by your deeds, Lord; I sing for joy at what your hands have done. How great are your works, Lord, how profound your thoughts!" —Psalm 92:4-5 (NIV)

DAY 1 *Joy*

Rejoice in The Lord always. I will say it again: Rejoice!... The Lord is near.
—Phil. 4:4 & 5b (NIV) The night my mom passed away was not humorous at all, but as I reflect on it, there was something funny about the ordinary moments that happened shortly before she took her last breath. We decided to take the breathing mask off because it wasn't helping... it was such a relief because it was so loud. Amidst our newfound quiet my sister started rustling through my mom's purse and pulled out some perfume. My mom loved perfume and my dad bought her beautiful, expensive bottles of perfume pretty much every Christmas.

"Should I spray it on her?" she asked my dad and me.

"No, " I kind of hissed and whispered.

"Yeah, yeah go ahead," my dad disagreed. So *puff*, out it squirts. My mom smiled while she lay there, which prompted my dad to say quickly, "Do it again." *Puff*, out it sprays on the other side. And the smile emerges again. "She likes it." We all agree and smile. *The Lord is very near now.* So, **joy** is sitting there with us right on top of her bed as the scene unfolds, and my sister and I argue about perfume like little kids.

Maybe an hour goes by and we're not sure how much longer we'll all be breathing together. My dad thought he'd go home and rest, while my sister and I stayed. He bent down and kissed my mom goodbye for the night, but also goodbye in the earthly time zone of forever. *That is what my mom was waiting for.* Understanding that joy and strength go together, the Lord gave my mom strength at that moment to lift her head and sort of breathe the words into his ear, "Good bye. I love you."

In her devotion on *Humility*, Michelle Simpson wrote, "**Joy** is knowing the Lord is near." Because my mom was with the Lord at that very moment, **joy** was more than near. It actually wrapped itself around my chest and lifted the pain that had lingered there for so long, due to my mom's physical suffering. Then **joy** took the hands of each family member and placed them together so that we found ourselves in a circle around the bed. We thanked the Lord for allowing my mom to achieve her lifelong goal: "*Be though faithful unto death and I will give thee a crown of life.*" —Revelation 2:10b (KJV)

Author Fred Bittner wrote, "**Joy** comes when we live in his presence." My mom lived in his presence. Both her life, and her death, brought great **joy**, even amidst great sorrow. And in that moment, I knew God was taking me another step down the road of adoption. He would use the loss of my mom to help me become a mom to someone else, my soon-to-be son, who had also lost his mom. It would be a **joyful** road because the Lord would be right there with me holding my hand, which would mean **joy** would be right there, too, holding the other one.

*Father, thank you for offering us **joy**, even in pain. Thank you for providing a crown of life to all those who are faithful. I want your **joy**, Father, always.*

DAY 2 //joy

Have you ever thought, "I think I could handle any trial except for _____"?
As soon as the words, or even the thought, is released you often regret it,
wishing there was an automatic delete key nearby. For me, the fill in the
blank was a major medical issue. I thought I could handle anything except
finding out that our newly adopted child had a major medical problem. But
there it was, this thought, floating in my mind like an unwanted balloon full
of helium. I wanted so badly to pop that balloon and see it whirl in the air
and then crash to the ground.

But it just kept floating.

I forgot all about the balloon for a while. We had been fostering in country for a couple months up to this point and the rest of my family had finally
arrived. Our precious little guy was now four-months-old. One night, my
husband and I were in the family room watching TV, holding our son as bed-
time approached. Suddenly we noticed something strange. Little B's mouth
opened and his tongue began to tremble. His eyed rolled upwards and his
little fists were clenched. "B, B, what's wrong baby?" We tried to calm him
and ourselves down.

Our immediate thought was that he had just had a seizure. That thought
was confirmed the following afternoon as we sat in a pediatric neurologist's
office. The doctor told us the size of our son's head was small and his mus-
cles were a bit rigid, signs of some abnormality. He needed an EEG and an
MRI. He prescribed medication and said he would need mental stimulation.

So there it was. The one thing I could not handle. And yet, there was
something else present. Something besides the tears and fears. Was this
joy? Again? *Consider it pure joy pure **joy**, my brothers and sisters, whenever
you face trials of many kinds, because you know that the testing of your faith
produces perseverance.* —James 1:2-3 (NIV)

Thoughts I never imagined I'd have in the midst of "the one trial I
thought I couldn't handle" began to surge. Thoughts like... "Thank you Lord
for prompting us to pray to be placed with the youngest child possible
before the adoption process even began. What a miracle that we received
him when he was only two-months-old! Especially after we had been told
it would be impossible to adopt any child under two- or three-*years* of age.
Thank you for placing our son in our arms before these seizures happened
so that we could be the ones to help him and care for him."

And so it happened. The one thing I had not considered when that unwanted balloon was unleashed. In the words of Fred Bittner, "**Joy** does not
depend upon our circumstance."

*God, forgive my fear. When I'm facing pain and heartache, thank you, Father,
for offering me something else... something better. Keep me focused on that
joy, knowing that with it comes strength and endurance.*

DAY 3 //joy

You make known to me the path of life; you will fill me with joy in your presence, with eternal pleasures at your right hand. —Psalm 16:11 (NIV)

The psalmist says God lets us know what path to take in life. He also says that when we take that path we will be filled with **joy**. So my husband and I asked God if he wanted us to take the path marked *patio* or *adoption*?

When we felt God urging us to consider the path marked adoption, we had $12,000 in our savings account. We are full-time missionaries. God has always provided funding for our needs, and many wants too, but we don't have a lot of extra money to play around with. Based on estimates I had read for international adoption, I didn't think our measly amount would even cover half of the expenses involved. Plus, we thought that money was going to be used to finish the patio we started building in our backyard.

But wouldn't you know it, I met with a friend who adopted two girls from the same country we were considering. For a slew of reasons, adoption costs for Nicaragua, at the time, were considerably lower than other countries. And, you guessed it, our initial estimates added up to about $12,000.

We continued to pray just to make sure he didn't want us to take the patio path... But for some reason it seemed that God cared more about children who didn't have parents than he did about our patio table resting comfortably on level ground. He answered prayer after prayer that pointed to the big sign marked adoption.

So when we arrived at the spot where the path split, we veered towards the sign labeled, "Adoption: A Lifelong Journey Ahead." If you were to retrace the steps on the path where we've already walked, you'll find that our journey, though bumpy at times, was filled with an overwhelming sense of joy because of the specific prayers God answered along the way.

Like the time I realized that there was a nearly $1,000 filing fee for a document I hadn't considered. But in went the check inside the envelope. And in went the envelope inside the mailbox.

At the same time, on the opposite end of the country, in went a check inside another envelope addressed *to us*. And in our mailbox, the day after I sent the check I had just written, landed that check with a letter. Inside were the words, "We were blessed with a bonus of $1,000 this month and God wants it to go towards your adoption." Those are moments that overwhelmed us with **joy**, knowing that we were walking with him in a very clear direction with a very intentional purpose. And although our patio is still unfinished, years later, those **joy**-filled moments remain. (I have a feeling we'll be blessed with some top notch landscaping at our eternal home.)

*Gracious Father, thank you for providing clear direction in our lives. Thank you for reminding us of your purpose. Help me hold on to that direction—and draw **joy** from it—regardless of my circumstances.*

DAY 4 //joy

"**Joy** comes when we spend our life praising God." —Fred Bittner

*Clap your hands, all you nations; shout to God with cries of **joy**. How awesome is The Lord Most High, the great King over all the earth. He subdued nations under us, peoples under our feet.* —Psalm 47:1-3 (NIV)

Have you ever felt surrounded by enemies? It's a scary and vulnerable position to be in. I felt like I was surrounded by "enemies" during our family's adoption process. The first enemies I encountered were not even real people. They were stories. Stories of adoptions gone wrong and stories of defeat and despair. Stories that made me want to run away and hide from all the unknown risks adoption could bring.

Some of my enemies actually were people. I remember one afternoon in particular. I was at my neighbor's house for a graduation party. While I was in line piling food on my plate, a lady ran up to me. I had never formally met her, but I knew she was the relative of a friend of mine. Without a hello or introduction of any kind, she just ran up to me and spat out, "Aren't you afraid of adopting. Aren't you afraid of letting someone else pick out your child?" *And now my head shall be lifted up above all my enemies all around me; Therefore I will offer sacrifices of **joy** in his tabernacle; I will sing, yes I will sing praises to The Lord.* —Psalm 27:6 (NKJV)

The Lord lifted my head in those moments and enabled me to say, "Yes, I'm terrified but thankfully God is in charge of matching us with our child." And because of the Lord's strength in those times, the entire adoption process became a sacrifice of **joy** as I quietly, earnestly offered up every step of the process over to him. *My lips will shout for joy when I sing praise to you—I whom you have delivered.* —Psalm 71:23. (NIV)

The third set of enemies were the governing bodies in charge of approving the adoption both at home and abroad. This is tricky to explain because they were not "enemies" who were hunting me down. It was easy to feel trapped by these governing bodies when I was confined to places and situations without the ink of their signatures and stamps of approval. I could not leave the foreign country where I was staying, nor truly call my darling baby my son, nor re-enter my homeland without their consent.

I felt trapped when I mistakenly viewed them as the final authority rather than God who can subdue nations and deliver his people. I wanted to ignore the enemies and instead choose **joy**. And so my most frequent and heartfelt prayer became…

*Lord, part this Red Sea of adoption. Take control of every person, every law, and every signature that rise like rushing waters threatening to drown me. Push them aside and create a clear, dry path that our family can walk across and be delivered to the Promised Land where we will legally be declared a family. And throughout it all, help me choose **joy**. No matter what.*

DAY 5 //joy

*For you make me glad by your deeds, Lord; I sing for **joy** at what your hands have done. How great are your works, Lord, how profound your thoughts!* — Psalm 92:4-5 (NIV)

I think the shepherds' response to the birth of baby Jesus mirrors what the psalmist says in the verses above. The shepherds went to see baby Jesus after the angels had appeared to them. Then finding that what the angels told them was indeed true, they left to spread the word about what had happened.

I never really noticed this part before, but after the shepherds spread the word, they went back to see Mary and Joseph again. On their return visit Luke 2:20 says:

"The shepherds returned, glorifying and praising God for all the things they had heard and seen, which were just as they had been told." They were showing their **joy** by continually praising God for what he had already done.

Mary showed **joy** by continually praising God a different way. Instead of vocally sharing the news, Luke 2:19 records that *"Mary treasured up all these things and pondered them in her heart."*

"**Joy** comes when we continually praise what God has already done." — Fred Bittner

I felt like I could completely relate to Mary when my precious Little B was placed in my arms by the director of the orphanage. *I was holding a miracle.* God had his hands upon this tiny baby who had been born so humbly thousands of miles away from me. I sent out this message shortly after receiving the news that we had been matched with our son:

"Thank you for your prayers regarding our adoption. We asked God for a boy as young as possible and after being told we'd most likely adopt a three-year-old, we now have a precious two-month-old son. We got a call only two weeks after our paperwork arrived in Nicaragua, that a situation had arisen in which a 40-day-old boy needed to be placed with a family immediately."

Though I sent out this message sharing our exciting news, all I could really do when I held my son was treasure up all these things that had happened and ponder them in my heart. I sat there considering the fact that this wasn't a miracle I was reading about in the Bible. This was an outright miracle that God performed in our family in the 21st century. And now, more than two years later, I still feel **joy** because I continually praise God for what he has already done.

Precious Savior, I cannot truly grasp the absolute miracle of your birth. And yet, you continue to work out all things according to your glorious plan, even in my life. Thank you, oh great and might One, for all that you have done and all that you are still doing.

disappointment

This week, we will focus on the **disappointment** we sometimes feel in adoption and parenting. Many parents pursue the adoption process after experiencing the grief of infertility only to wait for years to bring a child into their home. Others adopt an orphan of a different race only to later watch this son or daughter be rejected by family members and their classmates at school.

And still there are some who are silently grieving as it feels at times like they have adopted the most difficult person on the planet. They have spent years filling out adoption paperwork, raising money, and praying for their child only to find out that the child that God had for them is one who is frankly unpleasant. And worst of all, we so often are disappointed by the sin that we see in ourselves as we wade through the adoption process and as we parent our children. We always thought that we were patient people, but now we are disgusted by the sin that seeps out of our hearts on a daily basis.

Disappointment (especially once the child is adopted) is not too often talked about in adoption circles. Yet this subject does not go without mention in the Scriptures. The Bible has concrete hope and promises for those among us who are disheartened in the midst of adoption and parenting, which **STACY HARE** shares with us this week.

DAY 1 *//disappointment*

In your book were written, every one of them, the days that were formed for me, when as yet there were none of them. —Psalm 139:16 (ESV)

Everything ultimately submits to God.

In the beginning, God said "ocean" to *nothing* and suddenly massive bodies of water filled the Earth. Soon after, the world became filled with sin and so the Lord planned to destroy it. Wanting to preserve the animal kingdom that he had created, he instructed two of every kind of creature to walk into a boat, and they did. Jesus rebuked a storm, and water, which does not even have a brain or a will, obeyed him. Rulers of the earth also submit to God. The Lord hardened Pharaoh's heart and this powerful king refused to liberate the Israelite slaves. Through this God's power was manifested in bringing about the plagues. Even the Devil operates within the boundaries that God sets out for him as the Scriptures record Satan asking the Lord's permission before he could lay a finger on Job.

If God is sovereign over the elements, the animal kingdom, the rulers of the earth, and the Devil himself, will we then question his rule during our adoption process or long days parenting? Will we allow our minds to swirl into doubts, questioning, and even accuse God of wrong?

On really hard days—when **disappointment** seems plentiful—you may ask yourself if you should have adopted when you did, if you should have adopted this many children, from that particular country, or if even you should have adopted at all.

Do not let yourself conjure up scenarios that would make this journey "worth it" such as having a child who appreciates the sacrifices that you made or seeing your son or daughter grow up to love Jesus and maybe help orphans themselves. No, let your thoughts go back to the bedrock of the Word: *That every up and down in the adoption process, every sleepless night, every joy, and every sorrow in parenting was written down in the book of your life even before you were born.*

We cannot be sure of the rulings of judges or our children's future, but we can be certain that every detail of our life comes from the hand of a God that we can trust. Submit to and rest not in your circumstances but rather in your Sovereign God.

Sovereign ruler of the universe, your ways are simply higher than mine. Forgive my desires for an explanation regarding the circumstances that I face. I want to instead humbly bow to that which you have planned for me, trusting you like a child.

DAY 2 //disappointment

A thorn was given me in the flesh, a messenger of Satan to harass me... Three times I pleaded with the Lord about this, that it should leave me. But he said to me, "My grace is sufficient for you, for my power is made perfect in weakness."
—2 Corinthians 12:7-9a (ESV)

If only our adoption would go through, I would be happy. If I did not have to devote so much energy to this needy, difficult child I could be freed up to do more. If only I could go one day without yelling at my kids! Any of those statements sound familiar?

We, like Paul, look up to God and humbly ask for him to remove these trials from us. Often times, our Shepherd responds in saying *"my grace is sufficient for you, for my power is made perfect in weakness."*

That's **disappointing**, isn't it? Couldn't he just take away the pain?

The thing is, God's grace is *not* perfected in me when I accomplish everything on my to-do list or, when I graciously respond to my complaining three-year-old. No, God's power is most pronounced when we realize that we are weak. We cannot control governments, we cannot make our children love God, and we cannot stop sinning. Although the world and our flesh tell us that weakness is to be avoided at all costs, the Lord tells us that weakness is a position of power.

Power to do what?

God's grace is sufficient to give us the power to do good works especially in our weakest moments. 2 Corinthians 9:8 (ESV) says, *"And God is able to make all grace abound to you, **so that** having all sufficiency in all things at all times, **you may abound in every good work**."* The grace that God accords to suffering believers is not a grace that eases the pain, but is instead a grace that empowers the believer to abound in good works in the midst of the pain.

God's grace does not mean that I will feel like waking up in the morning for a day of hard work, but it does enable me to get out of bed and serve people all day. God's grace does not promise that my loved ones will not get sick or die, but it does mean I can bow down and worship with Job saying *"The Lord gave and the Lord has taken away; blessed be the name of the Lord."*

When facing the challenges of the day, let us bow the knee to God and ask him to make his power perfect in our weakness so that we can walk in the good works he has planned for us.

Father, I confess that I want this thorn in my flesh to be removed but I know that it is in my weakness that your power is most clearly manifested. I pray that you would increase and I would decrease and that your grace would abound to me today so that I can glorify you in doing good.

DAY 3 //disappointment

If you love those who love you, what benefit is that to you? For even sinners love those who love them. And if you do good to those who do good to you, what benefit is that to you? For even sinners do the same... But love your enemies, and do good, and lend, expecting nothing in return, and your reward will be great, and you will be sons of the Most High, for he is kind to the ungrateful and the evil. Be merciful, even as your Father is merciful. —Luke 6:32-33, 35-36 (ESV) In the midst of a long, **disappointing** season with one of our sons, I vented to my husband that I would really enjoy him if he would just stop screaming in my face and throwing tantrums all day. My jaw dropped when my husband coolly responded, "Yeah, everyone loves those who love them." I was expecting compassion. My husband reminded me that it is easy to love little cooing babies or obedient school-aged children, but even sinners can do that. True Christ-likeness means loving our children when they sin against us without regret.

Sometimes their actions towards us are so serious that they seem more like our enemies then our beloved children. It is frustrating and disappointing. *How* can we love them during these times? *By leaving justice to God.* I am freed up to love my child because I know that he will not "get away with" anything. I do not have to constantly remind him of his shortcomings or try to catch him in his lies. I can instead rest knowing that either he will pay for his sins on judgment day or his sins will be paid for by Christ.

Romans 2:6-8 (ESV) says, *"He will render to each one according to his works: to those who by patience in well-doing seek for glory and honor and immortality, he will give eternal life; but for those who are self-seeking and do not obey the truth, but obey unrighteousness, there will be wrath and fury."* Each of us will stand before King Jesus *independent of one another* to give account of our lives. Those who lived lives of faithful devotion to Christ will receive eternal life. But those who ignored God's love and did whatever they wanted, in disobedience to his Word, will endure an eternity of wrath. Thus, I can rest knowing that the Lord will perfectly judge my son for his actions and *I do not have to.*

Judgment is for tomorrow, grace is for today. God awaits the Day of Judgment while showering his children with grace. He freely gives rain and crops even to those who despise him. He gives breath even to those who use it to blaspheme him. He keeps our hearts beating, even those of us who use our strength to persecute his children. We are called to imitate the Lord's mercy in serving meals to ungrateful children, blessing a child who just screamed at us, and diligently praying that the Lord would save them... *expecting nothing in return.*

Righteous Father, you love your enemies and shower them with grace. Please help me to follow in your example in loving my children—no matter how they treat me—expecting nothing in return.

DAY 4 //disappointment

Until now you have asked nothing in my name. Ask, and you will receive, that your joy may be full. —John 16:24 (ESV)

The call to rest in God's sovereignty, to accept trials as a means of personal growth, and to love one's enemies should by no means leave the believer in a state of passivity. The greatest weapon we have in affecting change is the weapon of prayer. Jesus himself entices us with promises saying, *"Therefore I tell you, whatever you ask in prayer, believe that you have received it, and it will be yours"* (Mark 11:24 ESV).

Why is it that instead of hearing this promise and immediately making a list of what we want to ask Jesus for, we instead start qualifying his words to make his statement sound less extreme?

Ironically, this act of not taking his words at face value actually renders his promise powerless, for he said that we must *believe* in order to *receive*. Perhaps the reason why we are not seeing answers to prayer is because we are focusing on our problems and not on the power of God who has set slaves free and raised the dead to life.

I can testify to the fact that the Lord has abundantly answered so many prayers in my life. Time and time again people have told me that it would be impossible for me to do this or that and time and time again the Lord has done the impossible.

I remember hearing one pastor's wife describe how her young child had absolutely no self-control. This child was wreaking havoc on their family life and again and again she would cry out to God in desperation that he would work self-control in her daughter. Today, her daughter is grown and is the one characterized, more than all of her children, by self-control, personal disciple and time-management.

The Lord *did* hear her prayers and he answered them that her joy might be full.

Let us be like the persistent widow who will not stop asking until God gives us what we are asking for. Let us pray for more orphans to be adopted. Let us beg the Lord to open more countries to foreign adoption. Let us ask that the Lord would grow us in godliness—even amidst great **disappointment**—and for the salvation of our children. Let us pray in faith and endure in prayer.

King Jesus, I believe that you are inclined to give good gifts to me as your child. Work in me the same perseverance of the widow who would not stop asking for justice until the judge granted it to her.

DAY 5 //disappointment

The appointed time has grown very short. From now on, let those who have wives live as though they had none, and those who mourn as though they were not mourning, and those who rejoice as though they were not rejoicing, and those who buy as though they had no goods, and those who deal with the world as though they had no dealings with it. For the present form of this world is passing away. —1 Corinthians 7:29-31 (ESV)

God calls us to honor and respect our husbands, but then again he tells us to live as if we did not have husbands at all. The Lord instructs us to care for orphans, and yet we are to live as if we had no children. The Word tells us that there is a time for rejoicing along with a time for mourning, and yet Paul tells us that we are to conduct ourselves as if these times of joy and sorrow were not truly real. *Why?*

Because that which seems most real to us now is actually fading away and will soon disappear.

Soon Jesus will return and we will no longer be married. We will no longer be mothers. We will no longer have that difficult boss. We will no longer run errands or do laundry. Most everything that consumes our lives right now will be done away with and instead there will be only joy.

Psalm 16:11 says *"In your presence there is fullness of joy; at your right hand are pleasures forevermore."* When we enter into the presence of our Lord, we will be entering into eternal pleasures. In fact, we cannot even imagine that which the Lord has in store for us.

No longer will we have that challenging child or spouse to strive to love for if these difficult people are believers, they will be lovely. The difficulties we face in working to survive, in having bodies that do not function properly and in dying to ourselves in service to Christ will be a faith memory for we will be a part of a new Earth.

We, as mothers, are Christians first. We are children of light, we will inherit the earth, and we will worship King Jesus forever free from distractions, sin, and struggles. This day is coming soon.

So today, let us strive to set our minds on things above, realizing that the **disappointments** of the daily grind will soon be a thing of the past. In the words of Isaiah (25:8-9 ESV): *He will swallow up death forever; and the Lord GOD will wipe away tears from all faces, and the reproach of his people he will take away from all the earth, for the LORD has spoken. It will be said on that day, "Behold, this is our God; we have waited for him, that he might save us. This is the LORD; we have waited for him; let us be glad and rejoice in his salvation."*

Lord God, help me to embrace trials in my life, strive to love my enemies, and pray expecting you to answer while also living in the reality that these problems will soon fade away. I wait for you and long to be in your joyous presence.

hope

This week we focus on the topic of **hope** in infertility and domestic adoption. **Tammy Wondra** uses the story of Job combined with scriptures of 2 Corinthians and Romans 5 to remind us of the gift of **hope** that God has blessed us with. Even in times we lose hope during the long process of infertility and adoption, God is always behind the scenes with an even bigger plan for us, just like in the inspiring story of Job.

SCRIPTURE FOCUS

So we do not lose heart. Though our outer self is wasting away, our inner self is being renewed day by day. For this light momentary affliction is preparing for us an eternal weight of glory beyond all comparison, as we look not to the things that are seen but to the things that are unseen. For the things that are seen are transient, but the things that are unseen are eternal. —2 Corinthians 4:16-18 (ESV)

Through him we have also obtained access by faith into this grace in which we stand and we rejoice in our sufferings, knowing that suffering produces endurance, and endurance produces character and character produces hope and hope does not put us to shame, because God's love has been poured into our hearts through the Holy Spirit who has been given to us. —Romans 5:2-5 (ESV)

DAY 1 *Hope*

During our struggles with infertility and adoption, I often looked at it as walking down a rocky path. With each failed cycle and each of our seven failed matches with adoption, the rocks seemed to hit me harder each time. I began to lose **hope**.

It is hard to travel that rocky path without any **hope**. And yet, once we grab onto it and choose to not let go, **hope** is the one thing that no one can take away from us.

2 Corinthians says, *"For this light momentary affliction is preparing for us an eternal weight of glory beyond all comparison, as we look not to the things that are seen but to the things that are unseen."*

When we look at the story of Job, he suffered and he didn't know why. I'm sure with every suffering and every loss he felt, those rocks along the path seemed to get bigger and bigger. He was tested over and over again. He walked that rocky path but he never stopped. He kept walking on that path even when the rocks must have felt impassable. He could see the rocky path and the rocks upon it, but he couldn't see the end result.

Our focus needs to be on the path, but not on the rocks. Adoption is a hard road to travel but there is a purpose to every step of the path. There is a reason God chose us to be on this path. And even though we can't understand now, *it is good*.

The rocky path that led us to Hannah was hard. But when I look at my daughter and hold her in my arms, those rocks don't seem as big and rough to me anymore. I still know they were there. But there is a certain peace I have knowing God really did have a plan for us. Our special delivery became a reality when it all needed to happen at the right time.

Rugged, rocky paths can be just as beautiful as the most manicured garden path. Your journey is simply a different one—beautiful in its own right.

Dear God, please help me focus on the blessings you give me during this rocky path of adoption.

DAY 2 //hope

My dream has always been to be a mother, not just to have a child but be pregnant also. In 2011, we decided to try one more time before turning to adoption. I was overjoyed when I got a positive pregnancy test on my birthday. God not only answered my prayer of being a mom, but also my prayer of being pregnant. My due date was January 1, 2012.

A few days later, my world crashed as I found out I was miscarrying my babies.

What I didn't know at the time was that God was telling me with that positive pregnancy test that I indeed was going to be a mother but not in the way I thought. Nearly eight months after my positive test, our daughter was born. Her due date was within days of my due date had I not miscarried.

2 Corinthians says, "*For the things that are seen are transient, but the things that are unseen are eternal.*"

When Job was tested, he lost everything. He lost his property and his family, not to mention his personal suffering. He felt like his world had crashed. What he didn't know was that God would bless his latter part of life more than the first. *Did you catch that?* God blessed Job's latter part of his life MORE than the first. He lived to be an old man and saw his children and their children grow up. He lost everything but then gained so much more.

God had given me a gift. He had given me my dream of being pregnant and motherhood. For a few days I had a tremendous amount of **hope**. My whole world crashed a few days later but I could only see the present, not the future. I saw God's temporary gift, not the eternal.

God has a hand in this and is making something beautiful. It may not make sense now, but it will one day. It's easy to lose **hope** and become discouraged. God is watching you and hurting even more than you to see his child in so much pain. When God takes something from your grasp, he's not punishing you but merely opening your hands to receive something better.

Only the people who are capable of great sadness are capable of great joy.

God doesn't allow us to suffer for no reason. Even though the reason may be hidden in the mystery of his divine purpose, we must trust in him, as the God who does only what is right.

Dear God, please help me to realize you have a plan for me and although I may not see it, I know you have wonderful plans for me. Thank you for your guidance.

DAY 3 //hope

There were many times in our infertility and adoption journey that I asked myself "Why? Why me, God?" I think it's only human to ask God why we have to suffer. We don't understand why things don't come easy for us, especially when it seems to come easy for others. There were many times I asked God why other couples could be matched in a situation within weeks while six months later we were still impatiently waiting. It didn't seem fair at all.

Romans 5 says, "*We rejoice in our sufferings.*"

Now why would we actually rejoice in our sufferings?

Do you think Job questioned God? Of course he did. At one point, he demanded an explanation from God. He cried out to God asking why he had to suffer. What pained him the most was God's apparent alienation from him. He didn't understand why God was allowing this suffering to happen to him. Job didn't think it was fair he had to suffer so much.

It's easy to lose **hope** and ask "Why me?" But maybe sometimes we need to ask "*Why not me?*"

It clearly states in the Bible we will all suffer. (Refer to Ezekial 21:4 and John 16:33, for example.) Everybody will. There's no question about that. But everyone's suffering is different. Through my suffering I have learned to be stronger as a person, wife, mother, daughter, sister, friend. I'm becoming more sympathetic and more understanding. I'm learning to appreciate the moments with my daughter and family more, to appreciate every hug and encouragement I receive.

I'm blessed. I'm blessed God has chosen me and has given me enough strength to go through this process of infertility and adoption. Someday I'll know the true reasons why, but when I stop to consider it, I think I can begin to understand.

As it says in Romans 5, our suffering produces endurance, which produces character, which produces **hope**. God wants our suffering to bring us closer to him.

It is often said that God doesn't give us more than we can handle but that's not true. God gives us more than we can handle so we turn to him. Without suffering, we wouldn't need God. God brings us through it. What an amazing feeling to know God will always be there and help us.

Dear God, thank you for your wonderful blessings you give me. Thank you for the suffering I endure, which gives me the blessings you provide me and the blessings I don't deserve.

DAY 4 //hope

When we first got the email that we had been chosen by our daughter's birth mother, we were shocked and very confused. Due to the cost of this particular situation being thousands of dollars over our budget, we had requested our profile not to be submitted, not just once but twice.

God had other plans though.

We found out that through an error on the agency's part, our profile mistakenly had been submitted and we indeed had been chosen. We somehow had to raise thousands of dollars in few weeks around Christmas or risk losing this baby girl.

2 Corinthians tells us, *"For this light momentary affliction is preparing for us an eternal weight of glory beyond all comparison."*

When Job questioned God as to why he was suffering, he was confused and professed his innocence. He talked about his former happiness, wealth and honor. He was panicking as to why God would let him suffer. He didn't see the big picture. He only saw the brief suffering and he couldn't understand why God would allow this.

Likewise, we panicked. We didn't see the big picture. We were scared we wouldn't be able to raise the money in time. We didn't know what would happen and at times we questioned why God would put us in such a situation. There were seven other situations we had submitted our profile—all within our budget—only to not be chosen. Why weren't we chosen for those situations instead?

But the other situations weren't in God's plan. We prayed and even though we knew it seemed impossible, we trusted God had a plan and a reason. We were meant for this particular situation and baby. God once again showed us he was in charge and we were miraculously able to raise the money in time, almost to the exact dollar.

In the same manner, God was also there for Job and provided for him. Job was rewarded greatly for his faithfulness and devotion to God. Even when Job didn't understand, he trusted God, knew he had a plan and Job was rewarded for it.

God has a hand in every situation in our lives, especially on the rockiest paths of our lives. He is making something beautiful. It may not make sense now, but one day it will. That's the beauty of having **hope** in Christ.

Dear God, please help me to realize even what seems impossible is possible through you. Please help me to consider my "rocks" as building blocks to something even greater for me.

DAY 5 //hope

During our failed infertility treatments, I kept track of the number of days I had **hope** versus the number of days I felt much despair.

After a year of infertility treatments, I counted the days. During that year, I had 339 days of **hope** and 17 days of much despair. That's a lot of **hope**. Some days I only had a little **hope** and other days a lot of **hope**, but there were many more days of **hope** than despair.

Romans 5 says, "***Hope** does not put us to shame because God's love has been poured into our hearts.*"

Job had a lot of days of **hope**. Even when his friends questioned him and his faith, he still held on. Job did question God, but his days of **hope** far outnumbered his days of despair. Focusing on his faith and **hope** helped him win favor with God. God blessed him richly because of his faithfulness.

Having **hope** is a blessed thing. God wants us to have hope. **Hope** is mentioned 130 times in the King James Version of the Bible. Most people think **hope** is "hoping something will happen" but the biblical definition of **hope** is "confident expectation," an assurance regarding the things in our life that are unclear and unknown.

Walking the adoption journey, we know there is a lot of unknown. We never know when a situation will come up. We never know if today will be the day we get "the call." We stock up on kid stuff and decorate the bedroom and try to be as prepared as possible as we know any day our precious child may be coming home.

Every day we have **hope** and God loves us to have **hope**.

I want to close this week by encouraging you to focus on your days of **hope**… the **hope** that God gives you to withstand this journey. *There is always **hope**.* **Hope** is something you can never have taken away from you.

As figure skater and Olympic Gold Medalist Scott Hamilton once said "Adoption gives **hope** where there is no **hope**." When the world says we should give up, **hope** says we need to try one more time.

*Dear God, please help me to focus on the moments of encouragement and **hope** and not on the moments of despair. Thank you for the precious gift of **hope** you give me.*

depression

Depression can be a very normal response during a life transition such as adding a child to your family, either through birth or adoption. As the experience forces us outside of our comfort zone, we often don't have adequate coping mechanisms to handle all of the changes. As a result, it is easy to lose focus and feel lost.

This week, we'll look at where God is amidst our despair, and how we can respond to keep our focus on Christ. Having said that, it's important to note that this series of devotions is not a prescription to heal all cases of **depression**.

Situational **depression**, or adjustment disorder, is how doctors often refer to the inability to cope during major life changes like the loss of a loved one, changing your family structure (such as through birth/adoption or divorce), moving, or changing jobs. Each of us is unique, but symptoms often include feelings of hopelessness, difficulty sleeping, sadness, a tendency to cry more than usual, trouble concentrating, extra anxiety/worry, and a withdrawal from normal activities and relationships. Some people also have suicidal thoughts.

When someone experiences at least five such symptoms at once, for an extended period, in such a way that they impact the person's quality of life, the condition is more likely to be considered *clinical* in nature. Whereas many cases of situational **depression** will resolve on their own with regular exercise and sleeping habits, a well-balanced diet, and conversational support through loved ones and trained counselors, more serious cases of situational **depression** as well as clinical **depression** typically require additional assistance either through medication, psychotherapy, or both.

The concepts discussed in this week's devotion are geared more toward the adopting mom who is experiencing mild, situational **depression** as a result of her new family dynamics.

If your **depression** symptoms are affecting your ability to safely parent your child, or even if they are just affecting your ability to *live* safely, it is imperative that you seek help from a trained professional.

» Ask your primary care physician for a thorough exam, to rule out physical conditions that might be affecting your ability to cope.

» Contact your church or pastor for the names of trusted Christian counselors. (If you are abroad, ask for counselors who offer Skype counseling.)

» Visit **WWW.CELEBRATERECOVERY.COM** to find the nearest Celebrate Recovery support group.

» Reach out to trusted friends and loved ones to let them know you are hurting and ask them to walk with you through the process.

DAY 1 //depression

O Lord, the God who saves me, day and night I cry out before you. May my prayer come before you; turn your ear to my cry. For my soul is full of trouble... —Psalm 88: 1-3a (NIV)

There's no way to sugar coat it: the Psalmist wasn't feeling particularly happy when he wrote Psalm 88. I've only included the first three verses above, but the entire 18-verse psalm continues in that same vain. *I am confined and cannot escape; my eyes are dim with grief.* (v. 8b)

Unlike most of the other psalms, this one doesn't end with blessings or thanksgiving. In fact, verse 18 closes with this: *You have taken my companions and loved ones from me; the darkness is my closest friend.*

Most moms, if not all, can recall at least one time when we could identify with these words. **Depression** can occur after significant life changes like moving, the death of a loved one, or even changing jobs.

But it also has a tendency to sneak up on us when we least expect it.

I remember talking to one mom shortly after she returned to the U.S. with her adopted daughter from Nicaragua. "I just don't understand. I am finally home, together with my entire family, after five months abroad. And I finally have the daughter I've prayed for. This should be the happiest time of my life, right? So why am I **depressed**?"

My friend felt ashamed and embarrassed at her sad thoughts, even wondering how God could love her when she appeared so ungrateful. "I know God brought us through miracle after miracle to finalize our adoption. I know I should be so thankful, and I am... mostly."

The thing is, God's love is not dependent on our feelings or our circumstances. No matter what is going through your head today, God still loves you. We can cry out to him in the midst of pain and he understands every single tear, every single outburst. We don't have to try and hide it, or act like we can't be completely honest with him. Nor do we have to dance around the issue. God's a Big Guy. He can handle it.

Why, God, do you turn a deaf ear? Why do you make yourself scarce? For as long as I can remember I've been hurting; I've taken the worst you can hand out, and I've had it. (v. 13-15, The Message)

When these words ring true in your life, cry out to God. Seek him even when you want to run the other way, or rather especially when you want to run the other way. Take refuge in the fact that no matter what you're feeling, no matter how low you've sunk, his love follows you there.

He knows your pain, and even when you're tempting to think otherwise, he is right there loving you through it.

Creator God, forgive me for doubting your love. But, Father, sometimes when I'm in the thick of it, I just feel so unlovable... remind me that it's impossible to escape the depths of your love. Amen.

DAY 2 //depression

Stacy was one of the most prepared adoptive moms I encountered during our two-and-a half-years of living with and supporting adopting families in Nicaragua. She was a social worker by trade, and had previously completed another international adoption. She knew all about the alphabet soup that confuses and frustrates so many adopting families: PTSD (post-traumatic stress disorder), ADD (attention deficit disorder), SPD (sensory processing disorder), and FAS (fetal alcohol syndrome), just to name a few.

And yet, two months into her fostering process to adopt two young girls, she was completely spent. She told me she just didn't know if she could keep going. She had left her family to travel far away and adopt kids she had never met before... kids who didn't even like her. She was desperate to return home to her husband and other children (the ones who already loved her!). She wanted to get back to everything that was comfortable and safe to escape all that wasn't.

The **depression** that had seeped into her soul was clouding out the very reason she had started this whole process in the first place. When that happens, we must first look to Christ's example before doing anything else.

Jesus knows exactly how it feels to leave your home and go somewhere uncomfortable. He understands how frustrating it is when you try to love someone who doesn't yet know how to love you back. And he absolutely gets the desire to escape something that is hard.

"Father, if you are willing, take this cup from me; yet not my will but yours be done." —Luke 22:42 (NIV)

If Jesus is our model, and even he looked for a way out... then we are in good company.

Feeling **depressed**, lonely, frustrated, and exhausted is *not a sin*. We are, however, more likely to sin when we are feeling that way. We are also more likely to ignore God's leading and sink further into the darkness. To combat that tendency, we must remember that God's love has not disappeared. To the contrary, as we discussed yesterday, he *follows us* into the depths of our despair.

He is there with us... if only we *look* for him.

Heavenly Father, I know you're here with me, even though I don't always feel it. Help me to focus on your presence, and to see you in the everyday life happening around me. Show yourself to me, to keep me from getting lost in the darkness. Amen.

DAY 3 //depression

Adopting older children often involves a lot of heartache. Perhaps the child knew his birth parents, even living with them for years before tragedy struck. Or maybe he has spent a decade in an orphanage, never knowing the unconditional love of a parent. In either case, he likely will have trouble connecting with a new parent, making your job that much more challenging.

A few weeks, months, or even years into the process, you might find yourself questioning whether any of it makes any sense... or whether it's even worth it. When Jesus was faced with making the ultimate sacrifice for children who may not care or understand, even he asked if there might be another way.

He withdrew from them and knelt down and prayed, saying, "Father, if you are willing, remove this cup from me..." —Luke 22:41-42a

When you are in the thick of it, having heard things about your kids that you wish you could erase from your mind, or experienced enough pain to last a lifetime, it's completely normal—even expected—to look for a way out. No one wants to be stuck amidst the hurt.

The key, however, to actually finding the way into the light often feels like the complete opposite of what we want to do. If we are to follow Christ's model, we have to let go of our own desire to fix the pain, and place our future solely in the hands of our Creator.

"...nevertheless, not my will, but yours, be done." (v. 42b)

It is only when we recognize our inability to control or correct the situation that we can allow God to work. And when we let him take over...

There appeared to him an angel from heaven, strengthening him. (v. 43)

When Jesus was at perhaps his lowest point, crying out to God looking for a way out, he gave himself over completely to God's plan. *And God strengthened him.*

God loves us. He pursues us even into the depths of **depression** and darkness, seeking to light our way out. He is there, ever present in our need, if only we can look for him and give ourselves over to his perfect plan.

Then, *he will strengthen us.*

Heavenly Father, if you are willing, would you find a way out of this pain? If not, I trust you. I want your plan for my life, not mine. I see you. I know you are with me through this process. Please strengthen me to live out my life according to your will. Amen.

DAY 4 //depression

Sometimes during the adoption process, we find out about past trauma or abuse that horrifies us. It's impossible to imagine such painful events taking place to anyone, let alone a child you now call your own. *But what if those things did happen? To her... Oh, God, please don't let it be true!*

Even just recalling situations in which I've walked with adopting moms struggling through the tragedies of their child's past; even just thinking about it is enough to twist my stomach in knots. I think **depression** is often a sort of wrestling with God over the circumstances of our lives. In that process, we have the option of focusing on those terrible circumstances, or on how God is strengthening us.

I once heard an interesting story from Fred Rogers, the host of PBS's *Mr. Roger's Neighborhood.* He shared how his mom helped clarify his focus when facing trials, "When I was a boy and I would see scary things in the news, my mother would say to me, 'Look for the helpers. You will always find people who are helping.' To this day, especially in times of 'disaster,' I remember my mother's words and I am always comforted by realizing that there are still so many helpers—so many caring people in this world."

As Christians, we know God has indeed left one helper in particular. John 14:26 (NLT) tells us, *"But when the Father sends the Advocate as my representative—that is, the Holy Spirit—he will teach you everything and will remind you of everything I have told you."* Yesterday we read about the angel–helper who strengthened Jesus as he prepared to go to the cross. That same strength and encouragement is available to us in our times of need. All around us, the Holy Spirit is at work. Perhaps it is evident in an unexpected gift, a *no* that miraculously becomes a *yes,* or the comforting embrace of someone who understands.

Two are better than one, because they have a good reward for their toil. For if they fall, one will lift up his fellow. But woe to him who is alone when he falls and has not another to lift him up! Again, if two lie together, they keep warm, but how can one keep warm alone? And though a man might prevail against one who is alone, two will withstand him—a threefold cord is not quickly broken. —Ecc. 4:9-12 (ESV)

When **depression** threatens to sideline us, the community of helpers steps in to keep us in the game. But... *how will they know of our need unless we share it?* Recall the psalmist who wrote Psalm 88. He was wrestling through serious darkness when he cried out to God. And then there was Jesus, preparing to make the ultimate sacrifice, opening his heart to his Father. We need to be honest about our feelings, with our Creator *and* with those around us, so God can use his helpers to encourage and strength us.

God, thank you for sending us your helpers. Give me the words, so I might reach out when I need help, and then the eyes to see and ears to hear so as to not miss your helpers in action. Amen.

DAY 5 //depression

This week, we've been looking at ways in which **depression** can seep into the adoption process, to steal away joy. Not only that, I've shared how God's Word deals with that darkness.

In John 16:33, Jesus himself tells us how inevitable trouble like this is: "*I have told you these things, so that in me you may have peace. In this world you will have trouble.*" But he also tells us of something even stronger than the depths of darkness that threaten to swallow us: "*But take heart! I have overcome the world.*"

The grace and peace of Christ Jesus is absolutely greater than anything else in this world. He has adopted us as sons and daughter, heirs to his Kingdom and everything including that grace and peace.

My grace is sufficient for you, for my power is made perfect in weakness. —2 Cor. 12:9a

His grace is always greater than whatever mess I might find myself in.

I recall the first time I was asked what lesson God was teaching me as he brought me further outside my comfort zone (and eventually into the adoption care ministry in Nicaragua). My answer came so quickly it surprised me: *the depth of my selfishness.*

When I stop to ponder that selfishness, and all of the desperate need I found around me in Central America, I can easily slip into **depression**. But, if I tell you I've spent the past few years learning just what a mess I am, I must immediately follow that up by explaining what else **I'm learning: just how big God is to take care of my mess.**

No matter how much I fail or how low I sink, his grace, peace, and mercy will always cover me. *Always.* If we place our faith solely in Christ, there is absolutely nothing that can ever separate us from the power of his love.

We will have good days and bad. Remember that Christ is not the source or author of our trouble! And, we cannot allow the darkness to tempt us into thinking it can ever win.

Because the end of this story has already been written. "*But you belong to God, my dear children. You have already won a victory over those people, because the Spirit who lives in you is greater than the spirit who lives in the world.*" —1 John 4:4 (NLT)

Father, thank you for sending your Son to overcome the world. Thank you for being greater, stronger, and more perfect than the darkness. Thank you for forgiving my mess, and for covering it with your limitless grace. Amen.

failure

Who hasn't felt like a **failure**? It's pretty safe to say we've all been there more often than we'd like to admit, especially after becoming parents. The enemy loves to tell us how terrible we are and how we'll never succeed. But God's Word paints a completely different story, telling us we are wonderfully made in his glorious image. Even so, he knows we'll still struggle with feelings of inadequacy, so he gives us a beautiful picture of how to overcome those thoughts. This week, I'll use Psalm 145 to illustrate this story of grace and strength covering our weaknesses.

SCRIPTURE FOCUS //PSALM 145 (ESV)

I will extol you, my God and King, and bless your name forever and ever. Every day I will bless you and praise your name forever and ever. Great is the Lord and greatly to be praised, and his greatness is unsearchable.

One generation shall commend your works to another, and shall declare your mighty acts. On the glorious splendor of your majesty, and on your wondrous works, I will meditate. They shall speak of the might of your awesome deeds, and I will declare your greatness. They shall pour forth the fame of your abundant goodness and shall sing aloud of your righteousness.

The Lord is gracious and merciful, slow to anger and abounding in steadfast love. The Lord is good to all, and his mercy is over all that he has made.

All your works shall give thanks to you, O Lord, and all your saints shall bless you! They shall speak of the glory of your kingdom and tell of your power, to make known to the children of man your mighty deeds, and the glorious splendor of your kingdom. Your kingdom is an everlasting kingdom, and your dominion endures throughout all generations.

The Lord upholds all who are falling and raises up all who are bowed down. The eyes of all look to you, and you give them their food in due season.

You open your hand; you satisfy the desire of every living thing. The Lord is righteous in all his ways and kind in all his works. The Lord is near to all who call on him, to all who call on him in truth. He fulfills the desire of those who fear him; he also hears the cry and saves them. The Lord preserves all who love him, but the wicked he will destroy.

My mouth will speak the praise of the Lord, and let all flesh bless his holy name forever and ever.

DAY 1 //failure

When God first started putting adopting families in our path, I thought it was a fun distraction from the stress of living abroad. We had arrived in Nicaragua a few weeks prior, without much in the way of direction or purpose. But when we were introduced to a mom from Ohio adopting an orphan boy, the shared newness of our situations made for an instant connection.

We bonded over the frequent lack of running water, our love of coaching soccer, and this smiling infant who didn't seem to have a care in the world. There is an immense need for families to have emotional, physical, and spiritual support while adopting abroad. We felt God nudging us to walk alongside them and provide support for their needs.

So when this precious child's little smile was replaced by repeated seizures, it shouldn't come as a surprise that my new friend looked to me for guidance. No, what truly surprised me was the depth of **failure** I first felt when faced with her great need... the first "test" of our adoption care ministry. The irony was that my sister has epilepsy, and my daughter had seizures. I should know how to handle this! But, I was in the midst of my own culture shock, learning to live far from home and so, so far outside of my comfort zone.

Did I know any good pediatric neurologists here in this developing country? What's wrong with him? Was there epilepsy in his birth family? Will this affect his ability to walk, talk, and learn? What is his long-term prognosis? *I don't know! I don't have a clue! Oh Lord, why did you put me here if I can't help her!?* It would be the first of many, many times in our adoption care journey when I have felt completely inadequate for the task before me.

Have you ever felt that way? Have feelings of **failure** ever overwhelmed you such that you felt like the opposite of King Midas, where everything you touched turned to ruin? Are you feeling that way now? If so, this may sound crazy, but I suspect you might be exactly where God needs you to be. You're likely already familiar with 2 Cor. 12:9, which tells that his power is made perfect in our weakness. Even knowing this, our inadequacies typically bring us more despair then strength.

I've come to realize that these feelings of **failure** are not unlike other physical illnesses, in that they require a certain prescription to be healed. Thankfully, God has provided a set of instructions in his Word for overcoming the despair that comes from focusing on our inadequacies. We'll look more closely at what he tells us in Psalm 145 over the next few days. In the meantime, turn back a page to read through the entire Psalm 145 and soak up the glorious power and perfect strength embodied by our God.

*Oh Father, sometimes I feel like such a **failure**. I want to bring glory and honor to your name, and yet I feel so inadequate. Please guide me as I seek to overcome these feelings, and strengthen your power in me. Amen.*

DAY 2 //failure

We all fail.

A lot.

If you think you're the only one, you simply believe a sneaky lie of the devil. He loves to make us feel like we're all alone in our pain and torment. I think it is one of his most powerful weapons. But it's simply *not true*. Ever.

In parenting, no matter where the child(ren) come from, there's plenty of opportunities for **failure**. Yet, it's not exactly something we walk around sharing, as it causes us to buy into Satan's lies even more. We post about our kids' honor roll grades on social media, but not about the test scores that threaten to hold them back a year. Success is something to be promoted and praised, while **failure** is not.

David, the author of Psalm 145, heard all about God's works from his mother, who shared the ancient Scriptures to him before he could read them on his own. And in this psalm, he talks a lot about praising success, particularly in verses 4-7: *One generation shall commend your works to another, and shall declare your mighty acts. On the glorious splendor of your majesty, and on your wondrous works, I will meditate. They shall speak of the might of your awesome deeds, and I will declare your greatness. They shall pour forth the fame of your abundant goodness and shall sing aloud of your righteousness.*

The thing is, he speaks not about praising our own successes, but those of our Heavenly Father. Sure, you're probably thinking, but where are you going with this? Well, yesterday I mentioned 2 Corinthians 12:9, in which Paul tells us what more about this concept.

But he [God] said to me, "My grace is sufficient for you, for my power is made perfect in weakness." Therefore I will boast all the more gladly of my weaknesses, so that the power of Christ may rest upon me.

Paul had repeatedly asked God to take away his inadequacies, but he wasn't inclined to do so. So Paul decided to boast about those weaknesses (which we might call our **failures**) because they highlighted those very same wondrous works David spoke of in his psalms.

When we are weakest, when we feel like we can't do anything right, we are in the perfect spot for Christ's power to shine in and through us. We only need to make ourselves available to him.

*Heavenly Father, I offer myself to you—weaknesses and all—so your power can shine through me. I will boast of the glorious work you are performing in me, to share of your successes, even in the midst of my **failures**.*

DAY 3 //failure

I know women who have failed to conceive, participated in failed adoption placements, and then, when they finally did adopt a child, felt like a continual **failure** as a mom and wife. It's after such long streaks of supposed **failure** that we sometimes shake our fists at the sky and yell, "How much more, God? Can't we get a break here?"

The prophet Jeremiah must have felt the same. He was branded by just about all of his contemporaries as a complete and utter **failure**. He spent decades trying to convince people to change their sinful ways, but no one listened. Rabbi Mordecai Schreiber describes his lack of success like this: "Unlike Moses, he did not free his people from slavery and he did not bring them to the Promised Land. Unlike Samuel, he did not crown a King David over them. Unlike Elijah, he did not perform miracles such as reviving a dead child or bringing fire down from heaven. Unlike Isaiah, he did not prophesy the defeat of a foreign enemy, namely, Sennacherib, the Assyrian emperor, which came true. He died without any tangible accomplishments and, as was mentioned before, history remembers him as a broken old man who sits on the ruins of Jerusalem and cries (as depicted by many artists, most notably Rembrandt)."

Yikes. That's not exactly how I want to be remembered. So how did Jeremiah respond to his years of **failure**? He cursed the day he was born (Jeremiah 20:14) and complained to God about how unfair life was (Jeremiah 12:1-6). Sounds about right. The thing is, though, Jeremiah never gave up. Oh he threatened to and seems to have wished for the opportunity to give up. But despite the absence of success (or even a hint of it), he persevered in performing the task God laid before him.

In verses 10-13, Psalm 145 continues with our prescription for overcoming failure by reminding us that we're on the winning side: *All your works shall give thanks to you, O Lord, and all your saints shall bless you! They shall speak of the glory of your kingdom and tell of your power, to make known to the children of man your mighty deeds, and the glorious splendor of your kingdom. Your kingdom is an everlasting kingdom, and your dominion endures throughout all generations.*

We may feel like we're losing the battle, but God has already won the war. His kingdom is an everlasting kingdom! No matter what minor **failures** we endure, even 40 years of **failure** like Jeremiah, these **failures** are just a minor blip on the radar screen of a dominion that endures all generations. God's power and work has greater success then we could ever imagine.

*O Lord, thank you for the glory of your everlasting kingdom and the power of your mighty deeds. Thank you that my life is part of your dominion, even when I feel like a **failure**. Show me evidence of your glorious splendor, today, so I might focus on that instead of my inadequacies.*

DAY 4 //*failure*

"Mom, Anna is making the Lego people do weird things. You know, things only a husband and wife are supposed to do with each other?"

That's not exactly the conversation any parent looks forward to. So when my pre-teen daughter told me what the nine-year-old orphan-no-more was doing, I was no longer concerned about the boiling pot of spaghetti on the stove. Instead, I was focused on the raging emotions threatening to overflow in my heart. *What are you doing, God? Why did you bring me to this place, only to leave me absolutely clueless about how to respond? And why did you allow these horrible things to happen to this child?*

If there's only one thing I could tell parents who are getting ready to adopt, it is this: God uniquely prepares every single parent to handle what comes through adoption. You may not immediately feel it, but he absolutely equips you to specifically care for the child he places in your home, in the moments when you need it most.

Sometimes that means being quiet and asking God to show us the way. Sometimes it means asking for help even when we're embarrassed or hurt. And sometimes it means waiting on the Lord instead of trying to fix it alone. Psalm 145, verses 14-20, tell it like this: *The Lord upholds all who are falling and raises up all who are bowed down. The eyes of all look to you, and you give them their food in due season. You open your hand; you satisfy the desire of every living thing. The Lord is righteous in all his ways and kind in all his works. The Lord is near to all who call on him, to all who call on him in truth. He fulfills the desire of those who fear him; he also hears the cry and saves them. The Lord preserves all who love him, but the wicked he will destroy.*

God sustains us when we feel inadequate and raises us up when we acknowledge him as Lord of our lives. Check out verse 15 in particular: *"you give them their food in due season."* He equips us and meets our needs, not according to our own personal schedule, but when we need it most. Verse 16 says that he is kind, not sometimes, but in *all* his works.

Do you believe that today? Are you believing this for your life, not just now, but always? If we're going to get through this parenting thing, together, and make it out to the other side, we must accept God's Word as truth and allow his successes to overcome our **failures**. He wants us to bow down to him in our weakness, and allow his power and his strength to flow through, for ourselves and all those with whom we share life.

Father God, I believe you are kind and righteous in all your ways. But, I feel inadequate for this road you're asking me to walk. So I bow to you in reverent prayer, asking you to fill the gaps in my abilities, to enable me to adequately love and parent the child(ren) you've placed in my life and in my home. Thank you for equipping me for this road.

DAY 5 //failure

This week, we've been looking at God's prescription for overcoming feelings of **failure** and inadequacy. Will we fail? Absolutely. I'm a mess, most days, how about you?

Psalm 145 identifies a few key steps to work through those days (or weeks or months):

» Bow down to God as the Lord of your life. Accept his free gift of grace and mercy, through the sacrifice of his son, Jesus.

» Praise him for what he has done in your life and for what he is going to do, even when you can't see it now. Focus on the fact that God has already won the war, no matter if it feels like we're losing the battle.

» Share his successes with others, regardless of your weaknesses. And don't give up pursuing the task he has placed in front of you.

» Talk to God, because he hears you and wants to sustain you. Be quiet with him. Let him to direct, instead of forcing your own path.

» While waiting, practice the traits God models throughout Scripture.

That last step is perhaps the hardest. Isn't waiting always the worst? But verses 8-9 tell us, "*The Lord is gracious and merciful, slow to anger and abounding in steadfast love. The Lord is good to all, and his mercy is over all that he has made.*" I don't know about you, but when I'm feeling overwhelmed, and hopeless, I'm usually prone to the opposite of grace, mercy, patience, and kindness. Yet tucked into the middle of this beautiful psalm is a directive toward those exact characteristics.

When a friend asked for advice because she was being hit repeatedly by her orphan-no-more daughter, she and I both felt completely inadequate for how to respond. But the more we explored the situation, the more we realized how the child's actions were a direct result of her own feelings of inadequacies and **failure**. That's because our normal response to those feelings isn't exactly grace, love, or mercy.

The funny thing is, if we can force ourselves to practice those very same traits, *even in the midst of pain*, the whole situation is cast in a new light. I say "practice" because grace, love, and mercy aren't the sort of things you become good at overnight. And even if you are successful at displaying them in good times, most of us struggle during the tough times.

So we give *ourselves* grace and then try to reflect what our Heavenly Father has modeled for us: Being gracious and merciful, slow to anger, and abounding in steadfast love. What a beautiful way to transform our **failures** into one of his glorious works.

My Savior, my inadequacies so often leave me hopeless. Thank you for modeling a better way for me to turn from my despair and follow you. Give me strength to be gracious and merciful, patient, loving, and kind, in spite of my failures. Thank you for continuing this beautiful work in my life.

humility

This week, we focus on the topic of humility in adoption and parenting. **MICHELLE SIMPSON** uses Philippians 2:1-11 to remind us of our need for total surrender, both to Christ and to those He asked us to care for. As Michelle explains, there are many, many voices telling us to place ourselves first, particularly as moms. *Feeling overwhelmed by the needs of your family? You need a spa day!* Maybe so (and the Bible definitely speaks about our need for life-giving rest) but the truth is that God also gives another answer in Paul's letter to the church in Philippi: **humility**.

SCRIPTURE FOCUS //PHILIPPIANS 2:1-11 (NASB)

Therefore if there is any encouragement in Christ, if there is any consolation of love, if there is any fellowship of the Spirit, if any affection and compassion, make my joy complete by being of the same mind, maintaining the same love, united in spirit, intent on one purpose. Do nothing from selfishness or empty conceit, but with humility of mind regard one another as more important than yourselves; do not merely look out for your own personal interests, but also for the interests of others.

Have this attitude in yourselves which was also in Christ Jesus, who, although He existed in the form of God, did not regard equality with God a thing to be grasped, but emptied Himself, taking the form of a bond-servant, and being made in the likeness of men. Being found in appearance as a man, He humbled Himself by becoming obedient to the point of death, even death on a cross. For this reason also, God highly exalted Him, and bestowed on Him the name which is above every name, so that at the name of Jesus every knee will bow, of those who are in heaven and on earth and under the earth, and that every tongue will confess that Jesus Christ is Lord, to the glory of God the Father.

DAY 1 //humility

When I was 38 weeks pregnant with our second child, God placed a beautiful call on my life. He asked me to adopt. My husband and I were volunteering with a humanitarian aid organization that focused on the world's orphan crisis. Something inside me changed when I heard it said: *if all the orphans in the world held hands, they would reach around the world twice.* My heart broke, and I knew God had ushered us into His heart for the orphan.

Now that I'm on "the other side," it is plain to see how the truths of Philippians 2 have been at work as our family has grown. At the time we adopted Josiah, our son Isaac was 4 and our daughter Emma was 2½ and I felt inadequate at raising two small children, let alone three.

Many hardships faced us as we returned from China, but the truth found in Philippians 2 remained. Here was Paul, sitting in prison of all places, telling his friends about the unspeakable joy he'd found, and how his joy would be made complete if only they would be of like-mind, living out the knowledge that Christ is worth everything, *in life and in death.*

He also told them something that strikes to the heart of what it means to be a mom who lays down her life for her family: "*Do nothing from selfishness or empty conceit, but with humility of mind let each of you regard one another as more important than himself; do not merely look out for your own interests, but also for the interests of others. Have this attitude in yourselves which was also in Christ Jesus...*"

Paul then described Christ's humble attitude and tells us "Therefore, also God highly exalted Him..." (v. 9). Huh. God exalts those who put others first? Yes, God honors the selfless.

In the midst of the sleepless nights and a regressing oldest child and adapting youngest, God reminded me about what he had already done. Jesus came to serve in **humility**. He came to lay down his life.

And through our adoption journey, God was telling me to do the same.

He was asking me to do something that was impossible on my own, but that took me to the foot of the cross to find strength, rest, and adequacy in Christ alone.

I realize that God has taken me on a challenging road *because he loves me.* He wants me to live a life void of selfishness and conceit and to walk on this beautiful journey of adoption, where the humble are exalted and the servant is the greatest of all.

Dear God, help us find our life as we lose it for you.

DAY 2 //humility

There are many things I am good at doing and do you know something? I rarely do any of them! Sometimes I do not know how to cling to the truths of this passage when all three of my children have been screaming and fighting for hours and I just feel broken and alone. Humility is not always the first thing to manifest itself in my heart, but God gives grace to the humble, so that is where I want to be.

God loves me enough to make me weak because he is strong and I am his. There is an eternal purpose in this calling *and that is gain*.

So, that means I read this Philippians 2 passage over and over and over again.

Our adopted son, Josiah, laughs and learns and blows us away every day with how smart and resilient and curious he is. This little boy endured more in his first 20 months of life than I could fathom, yet he has attached to us and loves us and trusts us (mostly). But, an area of his life where grief and mistrust has most often manifested itself is sleep. For instance, I do not know what his nap times were like in his orphanage, but here, they are terrible. He needs them, but he does not *want* them and often wakes up screaming and screaming and screaming. On one specific day, he woke up screaming uncontrollably while I was re-reading Philippians 2:3-4.

Do nothing out of selfishness or empty conceit, but with **humility** *of mind let each of you regard one another as more important than himself; do not merely look out for your own personal interests, but also the interests of others.*

Even though I often just want the 'peace' that comes with 'peace and quiet,' God wants me to learn *true peace*—where nothing is done with selfishness or empty conceit while I am looking out for the interest of others, including a child who needs my comfort when he awakens, even if he doesn't realize it.

God desires for me to learn to walk in **humility** as he carries me onto completion. He wants me to lay down my life for my children with the same attitude Jesus had when he did it for me. The path of **humility** is hard, but *it is good* and it is conforming me more into the image of Christ. That is the big picture I long to remember every day, even in the midst of the small picture hardships.

Dear God, Please teach us to never trade the working of eternal purposes with the fleeting gains of temporary desires.

DAY 3 //humility

Earlier in the book of Philippians, Paul talks about being "filled with the fruit of righteousness which comes through Jesus Christ," so today I want to talk about some of the fruit God is growing in my heart as I walk this humbling journey of motherhood and adoption.

Within days of finalizing Josiah's adoption, heartbreak struck our family. While we were in China completing our adoption, we found out my husband's 31-year-old brother (who was in the hospital for a major surgery) was not going to survive.

After his funeral, we traveled hundreds of miles away from our families to find our home filled with water damage from busted pipes. My husband needed to return to work right away and I stood in our soggy house with three young children—one who had just lost everything he had ever known—alone and overwhelmed.

And I started reading Philippians 2 again.

Even as I was barely holding on, its words told me, "*with **humility** of mind let each of you regard one another as more important than himself...*" In the midst of my brokenness, God was asking me to remember that there is "encouragement in Christ," "consolation of love," "fellowship in the Spirit," and "affection and compassion." Christ is the only reason any of us are truly able to "do nothing from selfishness or empty conceit."

And so the hard, refining work of walking through this season with Christ's humble attitude began. I would love to say that I *always* care for my children with a gracious, surrendered heart. *I don't.*

But, the fruit of the moments that I do are beyond humbling and beautiful. When I lay next to a frightened Josiah in the middle of the night to remind him that he belongs or when I hold a struggling Emma's hand to remind her that she is cherished or when I move towards a defiant Isaac to remind him that he is loved unconditionally... this is when I move closer to living out the truths of Philippians 2.

The fruit of **humility** is the fruit Galatians 5:22 speaks about and it blesses my children and refines me with its beautiful breaking. It means that I am able to love when before I would retreat. It means that I learn to walk in joy in any circumstance when before joy was dependent on my circumstance. It means that I answer with patience when before I would answer in anger. I don't *always* do these things, but the fruit of **humility** is growing and I look forward to the day when the truth of Philippians 1:6 is completed in me: "*He who began a good work in you will perfect it until the day of Christ Jesus.*"

Dear God, Please grow the fruit of righteousness in our hearts for the good of our families and for your glory.

DAY 4 //Humility

There are countless messages in the world that tell me to live for my own ease and comfort, but that is not what Paul teaches. He teaches me to live a life of humility, and that true life is only found as I follow Christ's example in laying down my life for others for God's glory.

Jesus emptied and humbled himself, served, and submitted in obedience to the point of death for the salvation of sinners like you and me because he loves us. Jesus' obedience to walk the hard road led to my adoption as God's child and ultimately led to us adopting Josiah as our own.

Before we adopted Josiah, as a mom of two small children, I was convicted by how much time I spent coveting others. This sin is closely connected to what Paul calls "empty conceit." I coveted those I perceived to be 'natural moms.' I coveted other moms' community and help with their children. I coveted moms whose kids were good sleepers. I coveted people who went to movies. It seemed that all too often my heart was far from Christ's example explained in Philippians 2.

And sadly, sometimes I didn't care... because I just wanted motherhood to be easier!

Ease and comfort tried to lodge themselves as permanent idols in my life. But, God was too kind to leave my heart mired in idolatry. He led me in Christ's strength on his journey to the fatherless. His kindness led us to Josiah.

He could also be described as 'all-boy.' Josiah climbs and destroys and will take any opportunity you accidentally give him to play in the toilet. He is reminiscent of a combination of Bam-bam and Curious George, a mixture that is both endearing and exhausting! But, most of all, Josiah is a true treasure knit by our Creator. He is a treasure I would have never known if I would have continued to live for my own ease and comfort and one whose enjoyment I would have missed if I continued to live a covetous mom life, far from God's heart.

Christ's example is changing me from the independent, protective person I once was into the humble servant he has for me to be. All the ease and comfort of this world are worthless compared to holding our precious son in our arms and walking the hard road to the glory of God the Father.

Dear God, help us lay down the worthless idols of this world for the treasured children you have for us.

DAY 5 *Humility*

The day after we first held our sweet Josiah in our arms, we were given the opportunity to visit his orphanage, the place where he had spent most of the first 20 months of his life. My husband, Josiah, our translator, our driver, and I set out on the journey to his orphanage, made all the more adventurous by our driver's apparent disdain for driving anywhere near his lane.

While we were grateful to have this chance to be able to give Josiah some small pieces to what the first months of his life had been, I was also concerned that he may want to stay in the orphanage. After all, it was the only home he had ever known.

Every family's experience at their child's orphanage is different, but for us, we discovered that Josiah did not want any part of his old life. He was not interested in being there. He wanted his mama and dada. He wanted the freedom given him in being part of his forever family.

Looking back on our precious moments, I realize that I can learn an important lesson from Josiah in what it means to choose freedom. This is the same lesson the Apostle Paul is teaching his beloved church in Philippi. The way of Christ's **humility** is the way of freedom.

He is teaching them and me that selfishness, conceit, and pride have nothing in common with who Jesus is or who he has for me to be. Paul points me to Christ's example on the cross and he longs for believers to stand united in the one purpose of living for Christ. He even says in verse 2, "*make my joy complete by being of the same mind, maintaining the same love, united in spirit, intent on one purpose.*"

It *completes* Paul's joy to know his friends are walking in the selflessness and **humility** that only Christ can give. Selfishness and pride constantly call out to all of us, *but Christ gives a better way.*

When we came home with an almost-two-year-old Josiah, it was clear that he did not understand the depth of the truths of Philippians 2 or what it fully meant to want his new parents over everything else he had ever known. But, he already had an understanding of what it meant to be adopted into a family. He had already begun to feel safe and loved in our arms.

So, I will end this week in the same way I ended Day 1, with the reminder that God wants us to live a life void of selfishness and conceit, and to walk in the freedom only found in his Great Reversal on this beautiful journey of adoption... where the humble are exalted and the servant is the greatest of all.

Dear God, Let us walk in humility on the beautiful journey of adoption to the free life that only you can give.

anger

Adoption—and parenting—can sometimes light a fire under certain thoughts, so much so that before we know it our whole emotional well-being has gone up in flames. It's completely normal to have those feelings, including **anger**. For example, we have every reason to be angry at any situation that leaves a child orphaned. But what happens when we allow that to grow so much that we begin to feel angry because we've been given a child with "so many issues." If we're not careful, what started out as righteous indignation can quickly become something that threatens to squelch out the only Truth that can actually redeem the situation.

This week, **JULIE SWAIN** highlights one particular area in which us moms can be prone to **anger**, and uses God's Word to show up ways to help keep our thoughts in check.

SCRIPTURE FOCUS //PSALM 139:1-18 (ESV)

O Lord, you have searched me and known me! You know when I sit down and when I rise up; you discern my thoughts from afar. You search out my path and my lying down and are acquainted with all my ways. Even before a word is on my tongue, behold, O Lord, you know it altogether. You hem me in, behind and before, and lay your hand upon me. Such knowledge is too wonderful for me; it is high; I cannot attain it.

Where shall I go from your Spirit? Or where shall I flee from your presence? If I ascend to heaven, you are there! If I make my bed in Sheol, you are there! If I take the wings of the morning and dwell in the uttermost parts of the sea, even there your hand shall lead me, and your right hand shall hold me. If I say, "Surely the darkness shall cover me, and the light about me be night," even the darkness is not dark to you; the night is bright as the day, for darkness is as light with you. For you formed my inward parts; you knitted me together in my mother's womb. I praise you, for I am fearfully and wonderfully made.

Wonderful are your works; my soul knows it very well. My frame was not hidden from you, when I was being made in secret, intricately woven in the depths of the earth. Your eyes saw my unformed substance; in your book were written, every one of them, the days that were formed for me, when as yet there was none of them. How precious to me are your thoughts, O God! How vast is the sum of them! If I would count them, they are more than the sand. I awake, and I am still with you.

DAY 1 *Anger*

For you formed my inward parts; you knitted me together in my mother's womb. I praise you, for I am fearfully and wonderfully made. Wonderful are your works; my soul knows it very well. My frame was not hidden from you, when I was being made in secret, intricately woven in the depths of the earth. Your eyes saw my unformed substance; in your book were written, every one of them, the days that were formed for me, when as yet there was none of them.
—Psalm 139:13-16 (ESV)

Early in my first pregnancy, God flung my heart into Psalm 139 with a vengeance. He wanted my soul anchored to the knowledge that my children were formed and knitted together by a Creator who doesn't make mistakes.

These truths have been etched upon my heart through five years of pregnancies, parenting, and adoption. He has continued to be so sweet to remind me through all three of our children why Psalm 139 is the scripture to anchor our hearts in the midst of raising the children we have been entrusted to care for.

He has called us to care for children with unique and special needs. Without a shadow of a doubt, this is his design for our children and the call of our family. It is difficult to write about this specific topic, not because of shame or wanting to hide, but more because of how sharing some of the deepest struggles in one's life can fillet the heart wide open. His cup for us is different than what we would have imagined it would be. The cup he has given us is not easy, but is *any* really easy for the cup-holder to bear alone?

For those who don't feel ready for such a calling, find rest in the truth that God has searched you and knows you. He knows when you sit down, when you rise up. He discerns your thoughts from afar. He searches out your path, your lying down, and he is acquainted with all your ways. Even before a word is on your tongue, he knows it altogether.

My question to God, at times, has been, "God, are you sure you knew what you were doing when you chose me?" Sometimes the challenges my children have faced has resulted in a deep helplessness within me, displaying itself through **anger**. I want to fix what I am helpless to fix. I cannot make it easier for them, and this reality has sometimes felt like too much to bear. But God has encouraged me with Psalm 139, reminding me that he knew what he was doing when he formed our children, and he knew what he was doing when he called them to be ours'. Therefore, there is no place for **anger** about the calling he has bestowed on us. No matter how much we don't know, no matter how inept we feel for such a call as this, *God knows us.* And He makes no mistakes.

Lord, we praise you for making us in your image. We thank you that not one part of who we were made to be was outside of your sovereign goodness. We embrace your design for our lives. May we look to you for strength to parent our children with intentional care for these beautiful people you have created.

DAY 2 //anger

About four months into our daughter's adoption process, we were told that our oldest son, Bryson, was diagnosed with a sensory processing disorder. This is one of those moments as a parent that you can't sugarcoat. These are the moments when life is hard and we are either going to see reality through the lens of the Gospel, or we are going to see it through the lens of despair. By God's grace, Psalm 139 was already our anchor.

For you formed my inward parts; you knitted me together in my mother's womb. (v.13)

These beautiful truths flooded my heart as I received news that threatened to be bigger than his promises. *But it isn't.* And it never will be. This is why: Psalm 139 defines our son, not a medical label. His love and fine handiwork, in creating every little neuron from the top of his head to the tip of his toes, was done exactly as God intended. No mistakes. In the face of hardship, we must **reject** anger and, instead, trust our Creator.

I praise you, for I am fearfully and wonderfully made. Wonderful are your works; my soul knows it very well. (v. 14)

If I am not anchored in this scripture, I can easily start to question God. *How can you be good if you made my child this way?!* But God has revealed his goodness to us in creating our son just as he is for his eternal purposes. Bryson is not defined by what he cannot do and may never do. Having neurological processing challenges is merely one part of who he is, a beautiful tapestry of unique and incredible qualities that make him Bryson.

My frame was not hidden from you, when I was being made in secret, intricately woven in the depths of the earth. (v. 15)

I do not want to change him, for to do that would be to wish he were different than who God created him to be. To wish that he were different would be to want to somehow create him in a better way than God did. I want him to be who he is, to be who God designed him to be. I adore him in all of his ways, his quirks, what makes him tick. He is our delight. Instead of falling victim to **anger**, I must choose love. God is faithful.

Lord, root us in your Word that speaks the truth of your craftsmanship in creating your beloved people. Let us rest in the work of your hands. Help us to believe that not one part of who we were created to be was outside of your control. Give us strength to remember this when our children face challenges as they grow.

DAY 3 *Anger*

Does our family have hard days? Yes. I bet yours does, too. Are there times when I am moment-by-moment clinging to God's Word to remind me of what he promised in Psalm 139? Definitely. Are there days when I am angry at God and (repeatedly) ask him why? Of course. Are there times when I just wish that God's cup for us were easier? Absolutely. But are there also days that I embrace this cup, and truly would not change one thing even if I could? Yes. That is my hope for you and me both. *Your eyes saw my unformed substance; in your book were written, every one of them, the days that were formed for me, when as yet there was none of them.* (v. 16)

We live in a fallen and broken world. Jesus came to ultimately restore and make all things new. This we pray not only for the heart of our sons, but also in the life of our daughter. For she faces developmental delays, but this does not define her. Developmental delays and emotional trauma does not mean "broken." I have learned that expectations placed on an adopted child are crushing to not only the parents, but the child too.

It has taken more months than I would have ever imagined to bond with our daughter. We are in an attachment dance that will be a journey for the rest of our lives. I have had to let go of expectations of reaching a "new normal" within the first six months of coming home from China. I am now choosing to find joy in the reality of our unexpected "new normal," although it is filled with many unknowns. It might take years for her heart to really begin to feel "normal." We have to re-work our definition of "normal" and not let the **anger** of a broken world take over. We must trust that God has us exactly where we need to be. We can take great solace in God's beautiful design of weaving our lives together through his plan of adoption. Whatever your story is, embrace it. At the first hint of any **anger**, pray that God gives you the strength to see joy instead.

Tis' so much sweeter to rest in the truth of his sovereign plan than to believe that this is all a mistake, that by some horrible accident our children have special needs. It is freeing to realize that the struggles with attachment come from both directions, and that it is not just our daughter who needs to be changed by his grace. No one can understand why we are given certain circumstances in life, but we can only trust in his love and his way.

Our daughter was not a broken child being brought into a perfect, unbroken family. She came home to a place where the people within share in her brokenness. We will journey with her, all of us imperfect, and we wouldn't want it any other way.

Lord, thank you for loving us so much to give us this cup. Thank you for entrusting these beautiful, precious children into our care. Thank you for refining us in the ways you see fit. Thank you for how you display your glory through the broken, through your beloved.

DAY 4 //anger

Day by day, we are overwhelmed with thoughts that fill our minds. We tend to ruminate on the struggles, fears, opinions, doubts, and shame of our mistakes as flawed people caring for children with special needs and attachment struggles. These thoughts threaten to fill our minds until they seem like a crowded restaurant of negativity and **anger**. We care for these children who are dear to the heart of God. How can anything dear to the heart of God breed **anger**? It can't, it shouldn't!

How precious to me are your thoughts, O God! How vast is the sum of them! If I would count them, they are more than the sand. —Psalm 139:17

Psalm 139 gently reminds us that we must pursue God to hear his thoughts about us and about our children. He is the One that placed the call on our hearts. He called fully knowing how we were created. He knows our strengths and weaknesses as parents, and how we would handle parenting his unique children. Once we answer a call with a yes, God equips us with the toolbox we need for success, even when we feel inept.

If you feel angry at the circumstances you were given, pray for peace. It works! Every child is different, biological or adopted. Every special need of any child is individual to that specific child. There is no cookie cutter answer. We need God's thoughts to parent these precious ones well.

O Lord, you have searched me and known me! You know when I sit down and when I rise up; you discern my thoughts from afar. You search out my path and my lying down and are acquainted with all my ways. (v.1-3)

He knew every intimate detail of our days, and yet he still called us to join him in raising and loving these children. He formed our children knowing what their story would be, and he planned that all of our lives would intersect. And in the midst of that intersection, we sometimes want to throw up our hands asking God, "What were you thinking?!" What an honest question! He was thinking a lot when he chose for this to be the story of our families. Only in clinging to God's thoughtful knowledge of it all will we find rest.

True peace is found in the truth that he is a loving, sovereign Father who desires to reveal himself to us in the midst of the beautiful tapestry of his design in our families. While we may have moments of **anger** in the midst of the circumstances that God is using to grow us, there is such freedom in knowing that he makes no mistakes. He purposed these struggles and challenges to bring us closer to him. There can be no **anger** in that.

Lord, we often have days when many thoughts overwhelm us about our parenting these unique children. May we look to you and trust you. May we continue to see your calling as good and the perfect plan you have created for our lives to intersect by grace with the beautiful children you have blessed us to care for. Thank you for your design!

DAY 5 //anger

I praise you, for I am fearfully and wonderfully made. —Psalm 139:14

God created me. God created my spouse. God created my children. He is worthy of praise for that alone. His blessings abound. When **anger** tries to cloud the view, I must focus on the blessings. Abolish Satan and remember that God didn't just create us. He made us fearfully and wonderfully. For that, we will praise him. May this truth always result in worship to the Creator. In his craftsmanship of designing each and every one of us uniquely, he wants to bring us to the place where we have the opportunity to see that he alone is worthy of all glory, honor, and praise.

When God created Adam and Eve, he proclaimed that they were "very good." However, sin shattered the original mold. Since then, a brokenness brought by sin has been cast into each person he has formed.

Broken people have led to broken stories. We look at our children and ask why he didn't just fix the original mold, but instead has continued to make broken people. We would love to spare them the pain that brokenness brings. It is easy to be angry at God. *God, why won't you spare my babies the pain of a broken world?*

Maybe the answer to this question is that he desires for us to see what we are *apart from Him*, so we will turn to him to fix the brokenness and we will love him for his great rescue. That comes when we see that we are unable to control our situation, and that he alone can bring salvation and fullness of life. What a beautiful intentional design. We will always need him. We all are in desperate need of the Gospel.

As adoptive parents, we are invited into displaying the heart of God. We are invited to love a broken child, not because they have anything to offer us, but because they *are* us. We are broken people with broken stories, and we were fearfully and wonderfully created to receive the love of an Unbroken Father who desires to hold us in his arms and love us simply because he wants to. This is his design. When we look at our children, we must remember that we were created by the same hands as them, and we must praise our loving Father that he has brought each of us into his family and made us his own.

Lord, the work of your hands is good. May we embrace your design in creating us just as we are. May we praise your holy Name for how you have created us fearfully and wonderfully.

spiritual warfare

Whenever you attempt great things for God, know that you will experience spiritual warfare. Many of us move forward with adoption thinking that it is a good way to expand our family, but very few of us adopt solely to bring God glory and to reflect His love. However, Satan knows that adoption shouts out the gospel message without uttering a word and he is very much against that. You will experience spiritual warfare throughout the journey. Adoption tells God's Story of redemption and love, so of course Satan is going to assault anything that draws people to Christ. Adoption is one of the most visibly beautiful examples of what God has done for us. Christ moves us from helpless, alone, lost in a world of pain, and he gently cleanses us, lovingly forgives us, and makes us royalty! There really is no greater 'rags-to-riches' story than the story that every Bible-believing Christian has. You must remember that whenever you attempt anything great for God Satan will attack you.

This week, **GLORYA JORDAN** is not talking about spiritual warfare to scare you, but to prepare you. Similar to the flight attendant telling you that you might experience some turbulence, she is discussing this topic so we are not shocked by what is to come. You will learn how to recognize the battlefield, how to prepare for combat by practicing spiritual disciplines of wearing your armor & knowing scripture, and how to be victorious in spiritual warfare by using your armor and claiming the promises of God.

SCRIPTURE FOCUS //EPHESIANS 6:10–18 (ESV)

Finally, be strong in the Lord and in the strength of his might. Put on the whole armor of God that you may be able to stand against the schemes of the devil. For we do not wrestle against flesh and blood, but against the rulers, against the authorities, against the cosmic powers over this present darkness, against the spiritual forces of evil in the heavenly places. Therefore take up the whole armor of God that you may be able to withstand in the evil day, and having done all, to stand firm. Stand therefore, having fastened on the belt of truth, and having put on the breastplate of righteousness, and, as shoes for your feet, having put on the readiness given by the gospel of peace. In all circumstances take up the shield of faith, with which you can extinguish all the flaming darts of the evil one; and take the helmet of salvation, and the sword of the Spirit, which is the word of God, praying at all times in the Spirit, with all prayer and supplication. To that end keep alert with all perseverance, making supplication for all the saints.

DAY 1 //spiritual warfare

Be sober-minded; be watchful. Your adversary the devil prowls around like a roaring lion, seeking someone to devour. Resist him, firm in your faith, knowing that the same kinds of sufferings are being experienced by your brotherhood throughout the world. (1 Peter 5:8-9 ESV)

My friends told me to be prepared for **spiritual warfare** as we began our adoption process but I really did not understand what demonic combat might look like in daily life. Satan's whole goal is to destroy us (John 10:10). He knows that he has ultimately lost the war, yet he is desperately trying to win daily battles to bring us down, inflict great pain, and keep God from receiving the honor due his name.

Within two months of starting our adoption journey, an unprecedented Maryland hurricane caused a tree to fall on our house. A hurricane of that magnitude had not occurred in over fifty years! It generated an equally rare splitting of a tree that capsized on our roof. Later that year, I broke my hand and foot. Having been an athlete all my life, I never had a broken bone, and here I was, on a scooter, trying to care for three young boys with several injuries. That initial injury, and the ensuing chronic pain condition, meant I couldn't walk for over six months.

Our children were not being stimulated in school, they were disobedient and inactive at home, and completely unruly within our community of friends. I truly felt like the absolute worst mom in the world!

All of this put a heavy burden on our marriage and we found ourselves in counseling for the first time in over a decade of our once healthy and thriving union. Just as Satan isolated Eve in the garden to tempt her to stumble, I felt isolated through all the chaos, failing to recognize it as a ploy of the devil.

Many well-meaning friends said we should not adopt. We actually did take a short break from the home study process as it was physically too demanding for me. It was literally the hardest year of our lives and we just could not understand what in the world was going on. We took our eyes off Christ and failed to recognize that we were under serious spiritual attack.

Dear Lord, there are times when it feels like life will not let up, and one thing after another keeps piling on our plates. Help us to turn to you first. Help us to keep our eyes on you. Make us keenly aware of when circumstances in our lives are acts of war by Satan himself. May we never go into battle unaware of the battlefield or the enemy. Your Word tells us that, "The thief comes only to steal and kill and destroy." We know that you came that "we may have life and have it more abundantly" (John 10:10). Thank you, Jesus, for defeating Satan by your death on the cross. Thank you for going before us, for walking alongside us, and for carrying us through as champions to the finish line. Amen.

DAY 2 //spiritual warfare

Yesterday, I illustrated how we failed to see Satan's oppressive acts to keep us from living a life that reflects our great God. He was coming to obliterate our family, yet we did not see him as the ultimate enemy, so we were not prepared for the grenade thrown at us.

Businessman Ed Silvoso declared this about the American church, "The Church in the West today presents too easy a target for Satan. We do not believe we are at war. We do not know where the battleground is located, and, in spite of our weapons, they are neither loaded nor aimed at the right target. We are unaware of how vulnerable we are. We are better fitted for a parade than for an amphibious landing."

Whenever you attempt great things for God, know that you immediately walk into the devil's sphere of assault. Now, does this mean you should never venture to do anything great for God? Of course not! Attempting great things for God blesses your life here on earth, gives an eternal reward (Deuteronomy 28:1-14), unleashes his power and riches on your life, perfects your faith (James 2:14-18), draws all people to Christ and ultimately gives God glory (Matthew 5:16).

As people of faith, we demonstrate God's love by endeavoring to do great things for him out of obedience to his leading (John 4:19). Bible-believing, faith-filled Christians should be on the forefront of social justice issues (Micah 6:8). We must fight for those who cannot fight for themselves; protecting the lives of the unborn, preventing slavery, feeding the hungry, rescuing children being trafficked and caring for foster children and orphans. Christians should be the first ones meeting these cries for help caused by sin. Christ-followers ought to feel compulsion to love as Christ loved but we must be keenly aware that when we do, we enter the combat zone of the Prince of Darkness.

Although this may sound intimidating at first and make us want to shrink back (which is in fact exactly what Satan wants us to think and do) we must recall the promises of God. 2 Corinthians 4:17 (GWT) says, *"Our suffering is light and temporary and is producing for us an eternal glory that is greater than anything we can imagine."* Never forget that even the very worst earthly onslaught of **spiritual warfare** pales in comparison to the great rewards that await us in heaven.

Dear Lord, help me to recognize that Satan wants nothing more than to keep me from proclaiming your great Name and the eternal life you give. Increase my awareness of the adversary's tactics, lies, and sphere of influence as I prepare for battle. Help me to walk in the victory that you already have. Thank you that you will never leave me nor forsake me. Thank you, Lord, that I do not need to be strong in my own strength, but in yours. Thank you for your Word, your Spirit, and the reward of Heaven. Amen.

DAY 3 //spiritual warfare

Satan has three primary ways of attacking the Christian during **spiritual warfare**—deception, accusation, and temptation. When the enemy sends deception your way, it is an attempt to deceive you into believing something that is not true, about yourself or God's Word. Eve was deceived in the garden by her own lust of the flesh, the lust of her eyes, and the pride of life. First John 2:14b-17 (ESV) tells us, *"the Word of God abides in you, and you have overcome the evil one. Do not love the world or the things in the world. If anyone loves the world, the love of the Father is not in him. For all that is in the world—the desires of the flesh and the desires of the eyes and pride of life—is not from the Father but is from the world. And the world is passing away along with its desires, but whoever does the will of God abides forever."*

Our two weapons to deal with deception—the belt of truth (Eph. 6:14) and the sword of the Spirit (Eph. 6:17)—are the Word of God. The belt is meant to guard against an attack, while the sword is an offensive weapon, to slaughter the enemy. One of the many ways Satan attacks us is through our thinking. We get incorrect perceptions of God by listening to Satan. He tells us God doesn't love us and how worthless we are, or reminds us of a past *forgiven* sin. We tear down those lies by feeding on the truth of God's Word.

The second attack Satan uses is accusations. The devil is known as the *"accuser of the brethren"* (Rev. 12:10). Accusations sent our way are the "fiery darts" found in Ephesians 6:16. They lead to guilt and feelings of unworthiness, which weigh us down and tear us apart. This differs greatly from the Holy Spirit's conviction, which leads to repentance and restoration (2 Cor. 7:9-10). The shield of Faith is what we use to quench the fiery darts of the enemy (Eph. 6:16). To extinguish the fiery darts thrown our way, we must meditate on the truths of God's Word and his past goodness. We must build our faith by spending time with fellow Christians. Otherwise we are in a war, with very little protection, and we *will* get hit.

Even Satan knows the Word of God! But he uses it improperly to condemn and shame. Psalm 37:4 (ESV) says, *"Delight yourselves in the Lord and He will give you the desires of your heart."* Satan whispered continual lies to me that because of an act of rebellion I committed years ago, I would never get my heart's desire, even though I was currently walking in obedience! Obviously this is a gross distortion of God's promise but its' subtly was only recognizable with the discernment of the Holy Spirit. I had to stand on the righteousness of God through Jesus knowing that my past sin was forgiven. When God sees me, He sees Jesus, a perfect sacrificial lamb, who covered and took away my sin (I Peter 1:19).

Dear Jesus, thank you for your continued grace, mercy, and forgiveness. The enemy often tries to remind me of all the awful things that I've done. Thank you for washing it all away, and clothing me in your righteousness! Thank you for the ability to walk as a royal heir with Christ and for your goodness to me.

DAY 4 //spiritual warfare

The final tactic Satan uses in his **spiritual warfare** is temptation. *When tempted, no one should say, "God is tempting me." For God cannot be tempted by evil, nor does he tempt anyone; but each person is tempted when they are dragged away by their own evil desire and enticed. Then, after desire has conceived, it gives birth to sin; and sin, when it is full-grown, gives birth to death.* (James 1:13-15 NIV)

People will be drawn to sin when the enemy tries to convince them it is harmless. Jesus saw through Satan's deception in the wilderness. He resisted temptation by speaking God's Word. King David said in Psalm 119:11 (JUB), *"Thy Word have I hid in mine heart, that I might not sin against thee."* It's as if Satan shows you the worm, but behind the worm is a hook. The Word of God is our protection. We must memorize scripture and understand its context. Satan knows the Word and uses it improperly to attack, shame, and condemn us. We must stand firm on the promises of God.

In Romans 12:2 (JUB), we are told, *"be not conformed to this world: but be ye transformed by the renewing of your mind."* Renew your mind in God's Word! *"That he might sanctify and cleanse* [us] *with the washing of water by the Word."* (Eph. 5:26 JUB) We must have daily time with God's Word; encourage others in truth and love.

I shared some of the difficulties we encountered during our adoption process. Satan fed me continual lies of how I was a terrible mother, so why should I add more kids to my life? I wasn't prepared for these attacks. I didn't have truth to stand on, but God's faithful. He would often send others to speak truth into my life. I had friends encourage me to spend more time in the Word. They said to be quiet and hear His voice, not the lies I kept rehearsing in my head.

I am encouraging you to begin spiritual discipline. You may not know when you will need to begin the race, but it is imperative that you train for it anyway. In James 4:7, we are told to resist the devil and he will flee from us. But it's not that simple; in the same verse, we are also told to draw near to God. Dealing with temptation is a two-fold process. The closer you get to God, and the more you become aware of His love, the less power temptation will have over you.

The funny thing is, the more I depend on God, the more I accomplish in my daily life. The more time I spend in His Word, the more I get done in the remaining time I have. The closer I get to God, the less inclined I am to yell at my kids, to be quick to anger, or to rehearse the enemy's lies.

Dear Lord, help me to resist the temptations that surround my every side. Please allow me to avoid the traps laid before me. Help me submerge myself in your Truth, letting all else fade away. I pray for your strength to resist the devil. Thank you for promises that never fail. I praise you for never leaving or forsaking me. Amen.

DAY 5 *//spiritual warfare*

Put on the whole armor of God, that you may be able to stand against the schemes of the devil. —Ephesians 6:11 (ESV)

Our adoption went through the normal highs and lows. I went into the process cautiously optimistic, yet, at times, I literally felt like I was drowning and found myself in a particularly dark season. Around the time of my depression, I heard a sermon about feeling so overwhelmed you didn't think you could go on. The speaker told us to imagine ourselves lying on the floor of the ocean. The darkness found at the sea depths brought feelings of hopelessness that often accompany **spiritual warfare**. You were drowning, where you felt like you'd never make it to the surface for air. This was exactly how I felt. Days were spent doing life and adoption paperwork, only to have my home study rejected yet again. Every stress pushed me deeper.

The speaker continued, saying that although she felt like she was drowning, the Lord told her to stand on his promises and he would be faithful. She recited verses like Joshua 1:7-9 (ESV): *Only be strong and very courageous, being careful to do according to all the law that Moses my servant commanded you. Do not turn from it to the right hand or to the left, that you may have good success wherever you go. This Book of the Law shall not depart from your mouth, but you shall meditate on it day and night, so that you may be careful to do according to all that is written in it. For then you will make your way prosperous, and then you will have good success. Have I not commanded you? Be strong and courageous. Do not be frightened, and do not be dismayed, for the Lord your God is with you wherever you go.*

As she began to claim these promises for her life, she realized she wasn't really laying at the bottom of the ocean, but merely in a bathtub only half full! This changed her perspective. She was able to breathe, and recognized she had been allowing herself to drown. Were her problems instantly gone? No, but her mustard seed-sized faith allowed her to see those problems with a God-perspective, not a human lens. *Therefore take up the whole armor of God, that you may be able to withstand in the evil day, and having done all, to stand firm.* (Eph. 6:13 ESV). My sister, it is ok to take tiny steps of faith! It is ok to start a short daily devotional time, to pray for five minutes in the morning, and to meditate on only one verse for a week. In fact, it is the baby steps that must be taken before one is able to run.

As she pushed herself up in the tub, she looked at the Savior, not the circumstances. She stood, no longer drowning. She was able to encourage others who felt overwhelmed in a foot of bath water. Praise be to God, he has done the exact same thing for me and he longs to do the same for you.

You have already won the battle! Thank you that it isn't possible for me to drown. Even when life overwhelms me I know you will never let go. I will be victorious. I might not experience that full victory in this world, but you will always hold me. You love me. All glory be to God, the victory is your's alone!

purpose

This week we focus on the topic of God's purpose for us. **ANNE MARIE GOSNELL** uses Hebrews 12:1-2 and 7-11 to remind us that adoption and life experiences are used by God to further our sanctification in Christ. By running the race set before us and making hard choices, God works a miraculous transformation in our souls as he perfects our faith. God has a unique **purpose** for each of us!

SCRIPTURE FOCUS //HEBREWS 12: 1-2, 7-11 (HCSB)

Therefore, since we also have such a large cloud of witnesses surrounding us, let us lay aside every weight and the sin that so easily ensnares us. Let us run with endurance the race that lies before us, keeping our eyes on Jesus, the source and perfecter of our faith, who for the joy that lay before him endured a cross and despised the shame and has sat down at the right hand of God's throne.

Endure suffering as discipline: God is dealing with you as sons. For what son is there that a father does not discipline? But if you are without discipline—which all receive—then you are illegitimate children and not sons. Furthermore, we had natural fathers discipline us, and we respected them. Shouldn't we submit even more to the Father of spirits and live? For they disciplined us for a short time based on what seemed good to them, but he does it for our benefit, so that we can share his holiness. No discipline seems enjoyable at the time, but painful. Later on, however, it yields the fruit of peace and righteousness to those who have been trained by it.

DAY 1 //purpose

It was exciting! We were going to adopt! I started a Facebook group to keep family and friends up to date on what was going on. I told them when we had the investigations and inspections. Eventually everything quieted down.

We waited.

We waited.

On a day in January 2013, I remember posting in the Facebook group: "We're taking the crib down. I guess we'll put all of the baby stuff away."

Finally, I wrote an email to our adoption coordinator on the third Friday of September. I told her to remove our name from the pool. It had been too long of a wait. I needed to move on. My family needed to move on. I deleted the Facebook group telling everyone we had decided to not pursue adoption since it seemed that we weren't going to ever be given a child. That was Friday.

The next Monday the phone rang.

My husband was on the other end telling me that the adoption coordinator had wanted to see if we were serious about pulling our name because we had just been chosen as a potential family the same day she received my email.

Needless to say, I told him we would consider the child.

Hebrews 12:11 says, "*No discipline seems enjoyable at the time, but painful.*" Waiting for a desired event is not enjoyable. It's drudgery. It's the unknown. But it serves a **purpose**. The rest of the verse states, "*Later on, however, it yields the fruit of peace and righteousness to those who have been trained by it.*"

Adoption brings about a better life for everyone involved. The child adopted receives a forever home. The parents who adopt, and any siblings involved, are being trained so that the fruit of peace and righteousness might be yielded. Adoption is tough. It is not for the faint-hearted because there is a lot of discipline involved, but the yield is tenfold!

Dear God, give me the strength to endure the discipline of waiting for I know that you have fruit that you want to produce in me.

DAY 2 //*purpose*

When people see us, or hear what we have done I receive different comments. I hear:

You are so amazing to be doing this! You are an inspiration!

Oh, this little girl is so lucky to be a part of your family!

God bless you! You have done a wonderful thing!

I don't know what to think about such words. My life is boring. The kids and I do our thing each day. Daddy goes to work. We work around the house. I am an ordinary disciple who is following her God. That's all. But there are days when I want to tell those people, "If you think adoption is so great, YOU do it!"

During the first months of fostering before adoption, I was an emotional mess. We had good days. We had not-so-good days. I didn't know what to think and feel. I didn't FEEL excitement anymore or ooey-gooey love. Love was a *choice*. The child was a stranger. This seemed like glorified babysitting 24-7. And yet, I'm supposed to be a parent. She called me, "Mama." She smiled sweetly when she wanted something and threw a fit if told, "No."

There is not much that feels inspiring in that.

I believe in Jesus, which means I have been adopted into God's family. I don't think Jesus died on the cross because he was feeling ooey-gooey love for sinful people. I think he loved us with a *choice* knowing that his actions were what we needed in order to live a life free from the deathly damages of sin.

It's been through my sharing of raw emotions in conversations, and on my blog, that people begin to be enriched by our story. The comments do not necessarily change, but because people are being encouraged by my run, they, in turn, become my cheerleaders on the days when I need them most.

We who adopt have a race to run. It will take endurance and patience, skill and love. But a runner cannot win a race on her own. It takes a team. Those watching us, supporting us, and encouraging us see the **purpose** in what we are doing, even when we lose focus.

Dear God, thank you for the people with which you have surrounded me. Thank you for speaking encouragement to me through them.

DAY 3 //*purpose*

I've sat here for a good five minutes trying to think of some flowery, poetic way to speak about how our adoption interview went. But I can't. It was hard. And we made some tough decisions. Our DSS interviewer was wonderful. She was gracious and honest with us.

Until you are in the thick of it, you have no idea how you will respond or what you can handle in hard, intense situations. So for my husband and I to fill out a three-page check list on what types of "behaviors or conditions" we would be willing to take into our home was extremely difficult. On one hand we have two young children to protect, and on the other hand, if we were to have a third biological child with ANY of these conditions, we would all adapt and love the child anyway.

Therein lies the struggle. We have the opportunity to choose, yet how selfish shall we be? God still welcomes his sons and daughters despite the conditions they are in. We are adopted into the kingdom of heaven with crippled and sinfully disgusting souls. And yet he runs to us, swings us up into his arms, and plants a huge kiss on our cheek.

Since we have two young children, some items on the checklist were no brainers. But what about allergies? I might have to make adjustments, but we can do that. Diabetes? Again, we can make adjustments. Birthmarks? Sure. What about blindness? Deafness? Heart defect?

I welled up at this point of our conversation during the interview. We said we would take any child who might have mild forms of these conditions. And then my husband said, "*We would be willing to take a child who might only have a few weeks or months to live. Because even he needs a family.*" I added, "*That would be the hardest thing we would have to endure. But we'd make it.*"

Our interviewer stared at us. "*Seriously?*" she said. Yes, seriously.

Of course we prayed and hoped for the best-case scenario. But I must be willing to surrender my will to my Father's. Our **purpose** is to run our race in such a way that it glorifies him. We must keep our eyes on Jesus and allow him to perfect our families, regardless of what ails each of us.

*Dear God, your **purpose** in using events in my life is to transform me into the image of your Son. Help me to endure my cross, as Jesus endured his.*

DAY 4 //*purpose*

When we agreed to take this little girl into our home to be our own, I had no idea what we were doing. I've learned as the days pass that not only have we brought this two year old into our family, but we've also brought in her biological parents.

As this baby grows older we will have to deal with her questions and curiosities. I've tried to ignore these people, downplay their involvement, and even hide gifts they've given to her because I am fighting with them in my heart. *I am her new mother. I love her the way she ought be loved.* **They** *have done nothing, or at least very little, to love this child.*

And then the Voice, either through my sweet husband, or from deep in my heart tells me, *"These parents are people and they are hurting. They have eternal souls and make mistakes just like you do. In this case, they are about to lose their child because of their decisions."*

What if that mother had been me?

But life isn't about me, even though I have been dramatically making it appear that way. I have been battling selfish thoughts and attitudes since this little one joined us: attitudes towards her, toward her parents, and stress over changes in family structure. Jealousy, frustration, irritation, anger.

The author of Hebrews tells us that God disciplines us like an earthly father. He disciplines us because he wants us to be holy. There is a **purpose** behind my frustrations and I need the Lord to help me prune the sinful thoughts away from my soul.

All I can do is bow my heart toward a loving God and ask for forgiveness to wash over me time and time again. Every day I become slightly more broken as more sins are shown to me. God's been in my face quite a bit. And I deserved every minute of the discipline. I take joy in knowing that God has not given up on me.

I pray that the Lord would help me to always see my daughter, and her biological parents, through his eyes. The sins I have exhibited are no different than theirs. We are all broken. We all need Jesus.

Dear God, please help me to pray for my adopted child's biological family and please search my heart for sins that I need to deal with. Thank you for not giving up on me.

DAY 5 //*purpose*

I wonder if God grins and laughs as he spreads his wings over us at that point of brokenness when he knows we are at the end of everything we have. I can see him kindly shaking his head as he knowingly lifts us up with the strength of eagle's wings. God has a **purpose** for each person. *Each of us is to glorify him and make him known.* And He will always give us the strength to complete his purpose.

But instead of being excited because this adoption opportunity had finally come, I was filled with fear. *Lord, God what are you doing? What are you doing with me? What is your purpose? Do you really want us to adopt THIS specific child?*

I was frozen. Filled with doubts. We were given the chance to refuse. Doubts and fears flooded my soul, but I knew God held them in his hands. I *knew* he understood. The fear did not go away, but I knew I could face it with strength that did not belong to me.

I can change the world. You can change the world. *God wants us to turn the world upside down for him.* And in MY world, that means being broken enough to place my plans, schedules, rules, routines, homeschool, and 'four people family ways' aside; and turn our family into one of five. It is sacrificing the peace of certain family dynamics and relationships I had with my other children as they deal with a new sibling. It's dealing with tempers and tantrums on almost a daily basis. I may be weak, weary, frustrated, and tired, but it's nothing compared to the weakness of an innocent two-year-old who was alone in the world.

This is my **purpose**, my calling, at least for now. My family adopted a new member. It's a hard adjustment, but we aren't called to do the easy thing. This is the road I'm walking down right now. This is the plan. My life is short. I must get after it.

You have a road as well. *What is your **purpose**?* What is God's action plan for you?

Your God is real. Your God is coming. Your God has a plan for you. Your life is short. We, as a church, must get after it because heaven is coming fast. And what we are about to do here is urgent. It's more urgent than we could ever imagine.

I'm determined, with God's help, to change the world of at least one little girl. It is God's purpose for me. Whose life will you change?

*Dear God, please help me to find YOUR **purpose** for my family, adoption, and life. You, Jesus, are good. Help me to trust in you.*

waiting

We all know that adoption is full of waiting. There is paperwork and approvals with lots and lots of waiting mixed in. This week, **MELISSA STANEK** takes a deeper look at the topic of **waiting**. She considers Sara and Abraham's **waiting**, in Genesis, as well as several other scriptures that explore how God wants us to respond to **waiting**.

DAY 1 //waiting

Time lines are stupid. There, I said it. I thought I would like having one, but that is the farthest thing from the truth. Time lines give us some kind of control. But it is a false sense of control.

My day started just like any other day, with a kiss from my hubby, a yummy cup of coffee for the insides, and scripture reading for the soul. After dropping my husband off at work and the kids at school, I was off to a medical appointment. After I got back home, I checked Facebook and found out my friend Amy had received and accepted a referral from Poland.

My heart screamed for joy and excitement that she was one step closer to meeting her child. Oh, but then the sadness and tears. Along with those came the doubt and questions like, "Why them first?" "Why did our phone not ring?" "Why does it take so long?"

Because God didn't say "yes" yet.

Oh my heart longs to bring home our child! I know that God is in control and I have to remind myself of that daily (hourly?). I will continue to rest in his timing. I will continue to pray for peace in the **waiting**. I will continue to pray for strength, and to be carried through when I just don't want to wait any more. **Waiting** hurts.

Even as I write this, I realize just how self-centered I am. Lord, forgive me for being selfish and thinking only on how I am feeling in this moment. May the words of my mouth only glorify you. May I continue to remember what you spoke in Isaiah 55:9 (ESV), *"For as the heavens are higher than the earth, so are my ways higher than your ways and my thoughts than your thoughts."*

As I reflect back on what happened that day, I am reminded of the story of another couple who longed for a child, Abraham and Sara. Genesis 15, verse four (ISV) tells us, *"A message came from the LORD to him again: 'This one will not be your heir. Instead, the child who will be born to you will be your heir.'"* God made a promise to Abraham and Sara, just as he made a promise to me, that he would add to our families. The only catch: it was in his timing, not ours.

Lord, as Psalm 27 says, "Hear, O Lord, when I cry aloud; be gracious to me and answer me!" Forgive me when I want something now and you need me to wait a little longer. I long to do your will and be content the entire time. I ask that you give me strength and courage as I wait for you Lord. May this trial serve as a reminder to "wait for the Lord, be strong, and let your heart take courage wait for the Lord."

DAY 2 //waiting

Our family began to pray for four precious little children that desperately need a home. We prayed for them by name daily. We felt God would add them to our family. So, we accepted a referral for all four. That meant we would go from two to six kids in a matter of minutes! Our adoption agency just had to contact our social worker to approve the change from three to four children. We were told that it wasn't a big deal, and we'd quickly move on to the next step. *That is why what came next was like a blow to the head.*

The social worker told me I was insane to think that we were prepared for four more children, and that she was not going to approve it. *What did she say? That it would surely end in disaster?* How does one additional kid equal disaster? She didn't even ask any questions about the placement, only focused on the quantity of kids.

My heart sank and I just did not know what to do. *Destroy our family?* I thought God was in this? *Where is he? Are we wrong?* There were so many questions, with no answers in sight. We could envision these little ones in our home. We felt God moving us in that direction. My husband and I went to bed with the heaviest of hearts. Later, I woke to a number of things running through my head. I asked the Lord to speak to me, and then came upon these verses in Hebrews 10 while **waiting**:

> *So do not throw away your confidence; it will be richly rewarded. You need to persevere so that when you have done the will of God, you will receive what he has promised.* (verses 35-36 NIV)

And then these in Psalm 40 (verses 1-3a ESV):

> *I waited patiently for the Lord;*
> *he inclined to me and heard my cry.*
> *He drew me up from the pit of destruction,*
> *out of the miry bog,*
> *and set my feet upon a rock,*
> *making my steps secure.*
> *He put a new song in my mouth,*
> *a song of praise to our God.*

The Lord always provides, even with things seem impossible. We have to wait, with patience, and allow his will to be done. Did you know that the Latin word for patience refers to 'suffering'? Sometimes the Lord calls us to wait, *with suffering*. Even so, he hears our cries.

Lord I thank you that you love us. I thank you for trials. I long to have joy in the trials, as you would have for me. I pray you would give me a new song in my mouth. My heart is so heavy. I will repeat Hebrews 10: 35-36 until it is on my heart from memory. "So do not throw away your confidence; it will be richly rewarded. You need to persevere so that when you have done the will of God, you will receive what he has promised." Amen

DAY 3 //waiting

The days following our potential placement of four left us with no clear answers. We were given the option of starting over with a different social worker, but that required redoing 4-5 months worth of paperwork.

We prayed and asked God to make this decision for us. This was a very hard step to take. Do we fight and redo paperwork? Or do we see this as a door that is closing right before us? We wanted God's will, not our own. But dying to self is so hard, especially in a situation like this, when you're already in love with the kids, and see them as part of your family.

I just kept praying that God would make our way clear. We know he is not a God of confusion.

I lift up my eyes to the hills.
From where does my help come?
My help comes from the Lord,
who made heaven and earth. —Psalm 121:1-2 (ESV)

We decided to take a few days and not do anything to push a decision one way or the other. Any time I thought about it, I just prayed that God would make the decision for us. We were willing to fight for them, with everything we had, but only if that was what God wanted.

And then the phone rang. It was our agency. *What would they say?* As the words were spoken, my heart sank... and yet I was at peace. God made the decision for us. The social workers from our agency had decided that this was not going to be the children for us and that we needed to stop fighting. We accepted the decision.

As I reflect on that week of events, I am amazed by the Lord and his protection. I am sure that without him I would have gone crazy on the woman telling me I could handle five kids but not six! Instead, I decided to trust God and his plans for my family. It was hard. (Isn't **waiting** always hard?) Perhaps the worst part was that in *not* fighting for that placement, we didn't know what would happen to those four children halfway across the world.

And we know that for those who love God all things work together for good, for those who are called according to his purpose. —Romans 8:28 (ESV)

Truly being patient in waiting is losing ourselves in God's perfect will.

*Lord, I know you are in control. Give me strength in my **waiting**. Carry me when I can't go any farther and direct me when I can't see. May your will be done and my heart be at rest. Amen.*

DAY 4 //waiting

*Today I choose to be thankful for the **waiting**.*

The lessons learned along the journey would not be what they are if we did not have to wait. We usually want things to happen so fast. Yet most would agree that, when we wait on the Lord to provide, it is always better than when we force circumstances.

God showed me a number of times during the **waiting** that he wants me to persevere, to press on even when it is hard. Day after day, we waited for the phone to ring to get another referral. Oh, Father, why did you break our hearts?

I have something else for you.

But there's something more. Throughout Scripture, the Lord tells us to be thankful. Should we only be thankful when he answers us quickly? He speaks in 1 Thessalonians 5:18 (ESV), *"give thanks in all circumstances; for this is the will of God in Christ Jesus for you."*

When we choose to be thankful in the **waiting**, we noticed our hearts became especially broken for the fatherless. We were burdened to do something. James 1:27 (ESV) instructs, *"Religion that is pure and undefiled before God, the Father, is this: to visit orphans and widows in their affliction, and to keep oneself unstained from the world."*

God always uses our **waiting** for his glory, perhaps even more so when we thank him for it. Throughout our family's **waiting**, we found ourselves praying daily for the voiceless, speaking out for the fatherless. We joined a community team working to fill needs related to foster care, adoption, and orphans. None of this would have happened if we did not have to wait.

All the **waiting** gives us a time to focus on what the Lord has done, and to be thankful. He was the one that separated the water so the Israelites could walk across the river to safety, (Joshua 4) so of course he will clear the path for our journeys. I'm learning to have a deep desire to look for him in the midst of all the trials. I don't ever want to forget how the Lord has brought us out each time, and we are better for it.

So, even when longing for the phone to ring with another referral, I choose to rejoice in the **waiting** and seek the Lord.

Lord, thank you for providing blessings through the pain. Thank you that your Holy Spirit dwells within us. I am so thankful that you have shown me over and over what I can be thankful for in the mist of a trial. I ask that you would continue to do what only you can do and that is to take the pains and suffering of this life and make them all good. You are Who I need to look to. You are the one I need to cling to. Provide strength as only you can. Amen.

DAY 5 //waiting

Months went by with no word. Every few weeks, I would send an e-mail seeking another answer to the same question. "Any word on a child or two that fits our home?" The answer was consistent: "No, not yet, keep praying." I would log off the computer and go about my day. *Praying.*

This went on for months, until finally the call came. Would we be willing to take a child with some medical issues? After seeking the Lord's wisdom, we knew this was again something he wanted us to pursue. We accepted, which led to a different kind of **waiting**: the I-know-my-child's-name-and-face-now-when-can-we-meet-and-touch-and-love kind of **waiting**.

God was amazing during this time of **waiting,** as I wondered how we would be able to show this child God's love from so far away. God gave me the act of praying for my child. Praying for her was such a joyful and painful experience. The joy came easily in praying for our next child. The painful part was knowing she would go to bed without us another night. But over time, God replaced the painful thoughts with the joyful ones, as we eagerly anticipated the day she would be in our home.

We did not have to wait too long to meet her. The experience was one that we were not prepared for. Sure, we'd read all the books, but we had no idea what it would feel like to finally hold this precious child in our arms. She was so little, so sweet, and also so scared. I thought back to when God told Abraham and Sara to go, in Genesis 12 verse 1 (ESV), "*Now the Lord said to Abram, 'Go from your country and your kindred and your father's house to the land that I will show you.'*"

God did not give many details; he just said to go. Abraham and Sara needed to trust that God would provide and protect them. They had to wait for him to reveal his plan. Even if it took longer than they were expecting... Just like Abraham and Sara, we have to trust God daily to protect and provide.

A few days later, we had to leave our daughter behind, and then wait to be called back. This was pure pain, like none I'd ever felt before. Yet, in the half year that we waited to return for her, God took my pain and turned it into an even deeper desire to pray for her.

And since then, my prayer life has never been stronger. It took a lot of waiting, and even more waiting, but I finally learned the importance of trusting God with all of my desires. He knows exactly what is best for us, **waiting** and all.

Oh Lord, my heart longs to find joy in all trials. I want to trust you and your glorious plan. I know you will never leave us or forsake us, and I take such comfort in that. Amen.

endurance

This week **AMY BULTEMEIER** will be sharing about **endurance**, using Romans 5: 1-5. As followers of Christ, we long to someday hear the words from our Heavenly Father, "Well done, good and faithful servant." However, it's easy to lose sight of this goal, and wonder how we can continue the race. So what do we do when we find ourselves in a place where God has called us, but we begin to question our faith, lose hope, and search daily for peace and understanding? As Amy says, "We start praying for **endurance**!"

When she returned back in the United States after fostering two daughters in Nicaragua for several months, she says she experienced what psychologists call "compassion fatigue." She shares this week how certain key passages from Romans 5 help sustain her as an adoptive mother and Christ-follower.

SCRIPTURE FOCUS //ROMANS 5: 1-5 (NLT)

Therefore, since we have been made right in God's sight by faith, we have peace with God because of what Jesus Christ our Lord has done for us. Because of our faith, Christ has brought us into this place of undeserved privilege where we now stand, and we confidently and joyfully look forward to sharing God's glory.

*We can rejoice, too, when we run into problems and trials, for we know that they help us develop **endurance**. And **endurance** develops strength of character, and character strengthens our confident hope of salvation. And this hope will not lead to disappointment. For we know how dearly God loves us, because he has given us the Holy Spirit to fill our hearts with his love.*

DAY 1 *Endurance*

We were exactly twenty minutes from landing at the Managua, Nicaragua airport when the reality that our family was about to be forever changed had finally set into my heart. In the prior weeks, I had been so focused on preparing our family to live abroad that I refused to let myself think about what life would be like once I met our new daughters. As I watched my husband and two young sons navigate our twelve suitcases through an unfamiliar airport in a foreign land, I could no longer hold back tears. My confidence in God's plan wavered; I was seriously confused as to how I got here, and I prayed for him to calm my fears.

In the weeks after, our family landscape was forever changed as my faith was tested over and over again. Thankfully I was reminded of God's faithfulness and how he did calm my fears that day we arrived in Nicaragua.

Our tests and trials come in various forms, which months later seemed rather insignificant, but at the time stirred emotions in me unlike any I have ever known. Two weeks into our journey, I said good-bye to our youngest son and husband as they headed back to the United States. I had no idea when I would see them again and as if that was not heartbreaking enough, at the six week mark I sat in our half furnished apartment surrounded by three of my four beautiful children and I felt more alone than I had ever felt in my entire life. I found myself again wondering how I got to this place and I begged God for mercy.

Romans 5:3 tell us *"We can rejoice, too, when we run into problems and trials, for we know that they help us develop **endurance**."*

Even as I begged for mercy, God was building my **endurance**. And I need that to walk the path before me... to persevere in loving a little girl that is not ready to love me back, and to have confidence in parenting when I am tired and spent. The path, at times, can be lonely and dark. Yet, as I look back to the moments when we first met our girls, I see that God has been giving me what I need in order to do his will.

And even though I wasn't always happy about living in a foreign country, parenting children that spoke a different language, and feeling as though I was failing, I was able to rejoice in the fact that I was not alone. God gave me the hope and **endurance** to face each new day and he is still carrying me today.

*Dear Lord, I don't always understand the trials in the path you have set before me. Help me rejoice even when I don't understand. Give me the strength to keep going and use those trials to build **endurance** for what ever might come next. Amen*

DAY 2 //endurance

When I start focusing on all the things I cannot control, my hope begins to fade. Once my hope begins to fade, so does my **endurance**. In Romans 12:12 (ESV) Paul reminds us, *"Rejoice in hope, be patient in tribulation, be constant in prayer."*

We were about five weeks into our fostering period when I became frustrated with unanswered prayers. I was not being patient, nor was I allowing God to carry me during the trials I was facing. The sad part was that I had been there before in so many circumstances in life... maybe you have too?

Romans 5:5 reminds us that the hope we have been given in Jesus Christ will not lead us to disappointment. *"For we know how dearly God loves us, because he has given us the Holy Spirit to fill our hearts with his love."*

I have been a long distance runner my entire life. So, it was easy for me to look at our most recent adoption journey similar to the way I would look at one of my races. Long distance runners need **endurance** to finish the race, but with God's plan we don't always know the path set before us! There are times when we have little information to grasp onto or are stuck in an unpredictable part of the process.

I remember feeling like I was at mile five on a half marathon course, spinning my wheels without any idea whether the next mile marker even existed! In those moments, I didn't know if I still wanted to finish the particular race God had set before me...

Yet, as I parent children that have endured trauma, I learn more about what **endurance** can look like. I watch my oldest daughter struggle to navigate a new culture, a new family, and a completely new life, all while mourning the loss of her past. Do I even have what it takes to help her through? My comfort comes from knowing that God sends people to walk with us as we endure life trials. He heals our loneliness through those relationships. This is a gift I can give my children, especially as my daughter is learning to love... as she perseveres in running away from a traumatic past into the arms of a loving God and the new family he has given her.

I couldn't see the finish line when I was at mile marker five of an adoption process, and, today, I cannot see the finish line in healing past trauma for my children. But just like in any race, all we can do is keep going. Maybe you are waiting for the next mile marker; maybe you are tired and losing patience. Remember God is carrying you and he will make that path straight, giving you the **endurance** you need to keep going.

*Dear God, I pray that you continue to carry me and make my path straight. Help me to use this time to rejoice in hope and build my **endurance**. Amen*

DAY 3 *Endurance*

When we began our first adoption journey, we had no idea of how things would progress. We felt led to adopt from a particular country, but we also knew that there would be uncertainties with international adoption. I tried hard to not get fixated on the trials and time lines, but after we had waited for months to meet our son, we were told the adoption might not be able to continue. I was heartbroken at the idea of never meeting a child I had grown to love. I clearly remember telling my husband "we will never do this again; the emotional roller coaster is just too much." Imagine my joy when his adoption was approved a few months later and we were able to travel and bring our son home.

In a process where information is sometimes limited, one can begin to feel frustrated; that is where I found myself so many times during each of our adoptions.

For anyone who has already adopted a child or is in the process of adopting, you understand the battle of paperwork and the frustration of waiting. If your process includes living abroad you may also feel the heartache of missing family during travel. It took years of prayer before we understood that God was calling our family towards adoption again and a few more years before we chose to live obediently. Our hesitation came because we knew we would experience frustrated feelings and our faith would be tested. The second time around, I played out different scenarios in my head as to how things might go and for the most part, none of those scenarios played out, but different ones did.

When I found myself in the midst of these tests and trials, I chose to start my day thanking God for the words that gave me strength during our first adoption process. Living in a foreign country and adopting two children was a completely different experience than our first and I had many opportunities for my **endurance** to grow.

This verse from James 1:2-3 (NLT) became one I prayed over each morning, *"Dear brothers and sisters, when troubles come your way, consider it an opportunity for great joy. For you know that when your faith is tested, your **endurance** has a chance to grow."*

My prayers became more about growing my **endurance** than focusing on the circumstances. **Endurance** to fix my eyes on God and not my failures. **Endurance** to love children that had emotional scars. **Endurance** to simply get through each day living away from the other half of my family. **Endurance** to accept that God's plan was for me to be exactly where he placed me at that given time.

*Dear Lord, help me see beyond my circumstances. Help me to have peace and rejoice during these trials in my life. Lord, continue to build my **endurance** for the journey ahead. Amen*

DAY 4 //endurance

One of my greatest fears is that I will not be enough for my family. I have talked with dear friends, sweet sisters in Christ that also feel the same way. It doesn't matter if our children are biological, adopted, or step children, the fear of not being able to be enough for our children is real for so many parents.

As we grow our families we wonder... Will there be enough time, enough love, enough food, enough money, or enough patience for everyone in my family?

Maybe you have returned home. Maybe you have prayed for years for the child you are caring for and it's harder than you thought it would be. It doesn't matter where we are at in the journey or how we got there; we are unified in the reality that *what we are doing is hard.*

It is hard because sometimes we have to leave family at home, sometimes the children we are fostering don't understand us, sometimes we don't know when we will return home, and sometimes after we return home, we realize it was easier living in our children's birth country. Sometimes our new children don't love us back.

It is hard because we expect more of ourselves than we can possibly give. There are so many times as a parent that I continue to wonder if I will ever be enough. And as I **endure** the self-criticism and compare myself to other adoptive parents, I know I never will be.

Not because what I am doing is hard, but because God doesn't want me to do it alone.

And I am learning that it's okay that I am not enough for my family!

I easily forget that when my personal resources of time, love, food, money, and patience run out, God is there to do the rest. James reminds us in James 1:12 *"God blesses those who patiently **endure** testing and temptation. Afterward they will receive the crown of life that God has promised to those who love him."*

Let us not forget that God wants us to ask him for guidance, forgiveness, and love when we are tested. He wants us to look at the examples he has already given us and use those to offer the same things back to our children. And at the end of the day, when we go to bed tired and overwhelmed, feeling as though we were not enough, he wants us to know that *we don't have to be.* We don't have to be because he has already promised us the Crown of Life; gifts of grace, mercy, and forgiveness.

God is enough, so we don't have to be!

Dear Lord, thank you for the reminder that I don't have to be enough. Thank you for always providing my family with what we need and for giving me the greatest gift. Help me to offer myself and my family that gift of love each and every day. Amen

DAY 5 //endurance

Anytime I hit the pavement for a long distance run, I want to know the course map of where I am running. I like to see the finish line in order to pace myself for whatever lies ahead. I have always known exactly where I was headed and had a pretty good idea of how long it would take me to run the race. Sometimes I ended more tired than other times, but I have always been able to cross the finish line.

I was about eleven weeks into living in a foreign country adopting our two girls when I realized I had no idea when or even *if* there was a finish line ahead. At the start, I thought I knew what I was getting myself into, only to later find out there would be many, many added miles.

So many times in a day the phrase *"Dear God, just help me now"* would ring silently in my heart.

Yet, I knew there was another race I was running… one of obedience, learning, seeking, and growing closer to the One that loves me the most! It was about finding joy in the moment and learning to pray not for the trial to be removed, but for strength to continue.

Whenever I felt defeated, all **endurance** lost, God strengthened me. He answered one particular prayer that began the moment we met our girls. Before words were spoken or hugs exchanged, I could tell that life had hardened their young hearts and they had lost hope. I prayed their hearts would be open to hear God's promises and to know how much love surrounded them. On Easter morning I received an amazing gift as one of my new daughters showed me a window into her heart and began to accept the life before her. That answered prayer brought me such joy and renewed strength; it built the **endurance** needed to continue.

Colossians 1:11 (NLT) reminds us, *"We also pray that you will be strengthened with all his glorious power so you will have all the **endurance** and patience you need. May you be filled with joy."*

That strength and joy helps us build the **endurance** needed to run a different kind of race. It is the kind of race that Paul talks about when he addresses the church in Corinth, in 1 Corinthians 9:24 (ESV), *"Do you not know that in a race all the runners run, but only one receives the prize. So run that you may obtain it."*

Are you running to just finish the race or are you running the race to obtain the prize that our Heavenly Father has in store for us?

*Dear Lord, help me to not just run the race, but to remember that I am running for you Lord. Help me be patient in affliction, find joy and be strengthened so I can continue to learn from the trials and build **endurance** to run a great race. Amen*

loss

Many of us ponder the losses in our lives and think we would be better off without them. We sit in self-pity crying, "If only _____ hadn't happened in my life, I could do _____". Take heart! God word says, "*And we know that God causes all things to work together for good to those who love God, to those who are called according to his purpose.*" (Romans 8:28 NASB) Through this week **ALLISON SCHUMM** discusses the topic of **loss**, including why it exists, who has experienced it, and God's response. We will draw closer to God, while using him as our ultimate example of how to respond to children who come into our lives through foster care and adoption.

DAY 1 //loss

Loss is the cornerstone of our existence. The world was created perfect, but with the introduction of the first sin we have caused a downward spiral of continued **losses**. Adam and Eve disobeyed, and sin and evil entered into the world. Thankfully, we have a God who is not immune from the trauma caused by **loss**.

God has experienced great loss throughout creation, starting with the fall, causing the loss of communion with his creation, and again in his sacrifice of his son on the cross as atonement for sin.

We see, in Genesis 3:7-8 (NIV), Adam and Eve's response to their sin: *Then the eyes of both of them were opened, and they realized they were naked; so they sewed fig leaves together and made coverings for themselves. Then the man and his wife heard the sound of the Lord God as he was walking in the garden in the cool of the day, and they hid from the Lord God among the trees of the garden.*

We worship a God who first helped cover his creation after the fall. He sacrificed an animal as atonement for sin and covered them with clothing from the animal's skin. *The Lord God made garments of skin for Adam and his wife and clothed them.* (Genesis 3:21 NIV)

Then he made the ultimate sacrifice for the creation he loved so dearly. *He who did not spare his own Son, but delivered him up for us all, how shall he not with him also freely give us all things?* (Romans 8:32 KJB)

Not only has God experienced **loss**, but Jesus came to earth and *lived* **loss**. He showed great compassion to those who were grieving. When Jesus found out that Lazarus had died, he wept, fully knowing that Lazarus would live again. Jesus prayed, wept and sweat blood, fully knowing he would lose his life on the cross. And what was more painful than crucifixion? The **loss** of constant communion with the Father. *And at three in the afternoon Jesus cried out in a loud voice, "Eloi, Eloi, lama sabachthani?" (which means "My God, my God, why have you forsaken me?")* (Mark 15:34 NIV)

We can take great comfort in knowing we worship and love a God who knows **loss**, who was willing to love us so much that he himself suffered **loss** on our behalf.

But because of his great love for us, God, who is rich in mercy, made us alive with Christ even when we were dead in transgressions—it is by grace you have been saved. And God raised us up with Christ and seated us with him in the heavenly realms in Christ Jesus, in order that in the coming ages he might show the incomparable riches of his grace, expressed in his kindness to us in Christ Jesus. —Ephesians 2:4-7 (NIV)

*Dear God, it is only by your love and mercy that I am alive today. Thank you for covering my sin with your **loss**. Thank you for loving me enough.*

DAY 2 //loss

When Adam and Eve ate of the tree of knowledge of good and evil, God could have very easily said, "Forget it, you can't obey a simple command not to eat of one tree. I gave freedom to eat of every tree but one, and you didn't listen to me." He could have walked away and left us in our sin and misery, possibly to live forever, but he didn't.

Rather, God made a plan for redemption and adoption. Through his **loss**, he has given us a beautiful plan to redeem all of us back into fellowship and, even better, made it so that we are his children.

When the time came to completion, God sent his Son, born of a woman, born under the law, to redeem those under the law, so that we might receive adoption as sons. And because you are sons, God has sent the Spirit of his Son into our hearts, crying, "Abba, Father!" So you are no longer a slave but a son, and if a son, then an heir through God. —Galatians 4:4-7 (NIV)

Sadly, as beautiful as adoption is, it is also a picture of things that aren't the way they should be. Everything that God did shortly after the fall is an image for us portraying that things should be different, but that sin changed everything. God cursed the ground and thorns were brought forth; he clothed Adam and Eve, despite the fact that it was extremely unnatural. We see a rose as a symbol of absolute beauty, but it also reminds us of the fall, because of its thorns. The same applies every morning when we put on our clothes, because they are a reminder that God had to cover us after the fall.

The ultimate picture of the beauty that can come from God's extreme **loss** was the sacrifice of his Son so that we could be bought back and adopted as God's sons and daughters. When we get to heaven, everyone who is there will have made the choice to join God's family. In our sin and ugliness, God chose to wash us white as snow and make us family. It is that same glorious picture that we should offer our children in their loss and suffering.

God says, *"Be strong and courageous; don't be terrified or afraid of them. For it is the Lord your God who goes with you; he will not leave you or forsake you."* (Deuteronomy 31:6 HCSB)

This is exactly what our children need. We need to meet them where they are and love them when they are unlovable.

*Father, thank you for modeling grace and love even amidst great **loss**. Strengthen me as I try to mirror that same grace and love in my own family.*

DAY 3 //loss

Yesterday, we closed with God's promise to us that he will not leave Israel, nor forsake them, (Deuteronomy 31:6). In Hebrews 13:5 (HCSB), we are reminded that this promise applies to us as well: *Your life should be free from the love of money. Be satisfied with what you have, for he himself has said, I will never leave you or forsake you.*

I don't know about you, but I take great comfort knowing that I have a Savior who loves me and will not abandon me, because I can be very ugly and unlovable sometimes. Who isn't?

When Christ saves us, we can find freedom and comfort in the fact that it is forever. Our Savior was forsaken so that we wouldn't have to be. Jesus took the punishment we deserve—he experienced great **loss**—so God will never, ever forsake us.

It is marvelous that we have such a perfect hope in Christ. Remember Galatians 4:4-7? Jesus' being forsaken means adoption forever for us. This should be the same for any child God brings into our family: *It is forever!*

Adoption is a picture of Christ's love for the church. It starts off as a one-way street with a Savior's giving his entire life to redeem the broken race of men. It's been said that we don't adopt a child to be a redeemer, but we adopt because we have been redeemed. We are broken people, trying to help broken children heal from their loss. As we look at how our children (foster, adopted, or bio) have been affected by the changes in their lives, we also begin to recognize what changes have occurred in our lives, physically and spiritually, to make us who we are today and who we are growing into tomorrow. By helping our children, we can learn to grow closer to our Heavenly Father and better understand our roles in his family.

Take comfort in your God, and bring this same comfort to your children. Each one needs to know, deep down in his being, that you will *always* be there for him, no matter what, regardless of the decisions he has made. God doesn't always agree with our decisions, but he doesn't ever walk away; in fact he chases the one in 99 that has gone astray! *"I tell you, in the same way, there will be more joy in heaven over one sinner who repents than over 99 righteous people who don't need repentance."* (Luke 15:7 HCSB) In the same way, we can love our children, seek their hearts when they go astray, and rejoice in the victories in their lives.

Gracious Father, thank you for always pursuing me, even when I have gone astray. Grow me in love and mercy so I might also relentlessly pursue the children you have given me.

DAY 4 //loss

In the midst of the greatest loss in Jesus' life, he showed the world great compassion. He was beat, spit upon, and hung on a tree to die, though he was completely innocent of all charges against him. Even Pilate could find no fault in him. Luke 23:4 (HCSB) states, *"Pilate then told the chief priests and the crowds, 'I find no grounds for charging this man.'"*

It was written into God's plan well before Jesus was sent to earth to fulfill that plan. As part of today's devotion, I encourage you to read Isaiah 53, the prophecy of Jesus' death on the cross and the reason God chose more **loss**, ultimately, to bring great glory to himself. Isaiah 53 (HCSB) closes with, *"He submitted himself to death, and was counted among the rebels; yet he bore the sin of many and interceded for the rebels."* How many of our children would you consider to be rebels? I can honestly say I'm a rebel, a sinner, and unworthy of grace! And my Jesus, the one who died on the cross for this rebel, intercedes for me, for you, for all!

Fast-forward to the day predicted in Isaiah 53, and there is so much more we can learn from our Savior. Through it all, Jesus' request before God in his suffering and **loss** is a beautiful, simple plea. He doesn't ask to be saved from their mocking, or relieved from the agony, but instead he focuses his attention on us, the sinful rebels who put him on the cross... *"Father, forgive them for they do not know what they are doing."* (from Luke 23:34 HCSB)

This is exactly the way we should look at adoption and the hurting children in our lives. Forgive the biological parents for their abuse, neglect, drug use. They don't know what they are doing, they are only living what they have seen. Forgive our children for their misbehavior, caused by the countless **losses** in their short lives, for they don't know what they are doing. In both instances, the abuse and behavior come from the downward spiral of **loss** brought forth after the fall.

Jesus interceded for us through his suffering on the cross, saying, "Forgive them..." It's our job, through our imperfection, to do the same. We need to be on our knees, before God, interceding on behalf of our children, because the abuse and resulting behavior... it isn't their fault. And it is our job to learn to meet them right where they are: Dirty, ugly and unlovable, and right where God met you.

*My Savior, I don't deserve your love, and yet you bathe me in it minute by minute. You forgive me, no matter the cost. To say thank you seems to pale in comparison to the **losses** you have encountered on my behalf. Guide me as I seek to forgive all those who've contributed to the **losses** in my child's life, and to love them as you love me.*

DAY 5 //loss

As we wrap up this week, I want to draw attention to the fact that God has given us a clear answer on how to respond to **loss**. Our God is not an impersonal God who has never experienced pain and **loss**. He chose to live suffering and **loss**, so he can relate to us. We cannot shake our fists at God and say, "You don't understand!" Not only does God understand, he also made a way for us to be redeemed, through adoption. Jesus, though suffering, begged God for forgiveness for sin for those who mocked and spit upon him.

Even so, what happens when it's hard? When we just can't do it anymore? Friend you are not alone even in this! Your savior knows! "'*Father, if you are willing, remove this cup from Me; yet not My will, but yours be done.' Now an angel from heaven appeared to Him, strengthening Him. And being in agony He was praying very fervently; and His sweat became like drops of blood, falling down upon the ground.*" (Luke 22:42-44 NASB) Jesus was in such agony knowing what was ahead of him, that he sweat blood. So he prayed to ask for a change in circumstances, while he was fully willing to submit to the will of God.

We are never promised an easy road. In fact, it is quite the contrary. James 1:12 (HCSB) tells us that "*A man who endures trials is blessed, because when he passes the test he will receive the crown of life that God has promised to those who love him.*"

We have learned that God has stepped into our world and experienced **loss**, both as God the Father and God the Son. We also learned about God's response to **loss**: *I will never leave you nor forsake you, forgive them for they don't know what they are doing, I will love you even when you are unlovable,* and, ultimately, *I will adopt you into my family.* Throughout the Bible, we are told why the world isn't like it is supposed to be and how God responded to the fall. We are to model Godly behavior because he is the ultimate example of what we should strive towards.

We also cannot overlook God's heart and response to the orphan. There are 43 verses expressing his desire to care for the fatherless. We have been given the most beautiful picture to learn from and model for our children. It is when our children see the same love and compassion that God has shown us that they will be able to begin to heal from their extreme **losses** in life.

Just as Jesus has loved us, we can show our children this picture through our response to them: I love you no matter what. I will never leave you or forsake you. I will intercede for you. I will always listen to you. I will stand at the door and knock. Your voice is important to me.

O Gracious and Loving Lord, thank you for the beautiful picture of love you've given us. I pray that I might be able to model that same love for my children, that they might know your relentless love and serve you with their lives.

providence

Many adopting families struggle with questions about God's providence. Will he really supply all of our needs? This week, **MARY OSTYN** shares what she learned about God's **providence** in the process of adopting six children.

SCRIPTURE FOCUS //EXODUS 14:10-31 (NASB)

As Pharaoh drew near, the sons of Israel looked, and behold, the Egyptians were marching after them, and they became very frightened; so the sons of Israel cried out to the Lord. Then they said to Moses, "Is it because there were no graves in Egypt that you have taken us away to die in the wilderness? Why have you dealt with us in this way, bringing us out of Egypt? Is this not the word that we spoke to you in Egypt, saying, 'Leave us alone that we may serve the Egyptians'? For it would have been better for us to serve the Egyptians than to die in the wilderness."

But Moses said to the people, "Do not fear! Stand by and see the salvation of the Lord which He will accomplish for you today; for the Egyptians whom you have seen today, you will never see them again forever. The Lord will fight for you while you keep silent."

Then the Lord said to Moses, "Why are you crying out to Me? Tell the sons of Israel to go forward. As for you, lift up your staff and stretch out your hand over the sea and divide it, and the sons of Israel shall go through the midst of the sea on dry land. As for Me, behold, I will harden the hearts of the Egyptians so that they will go in after them; and I will be honored through Pharaoh and all his army, through his chariots and his horsemen. Then the Egyptians will know that I am the Lord, when I am honored through Pharaoh, through his chariots and his horsemen."

The angel of God, who had been going before the camp of Israel, moved and went behind them; and the pillar of cloud moved from before them and stood behind them. So it came between the camp of Egypt and the camp of

Israel; and there was the cloud along with the darkness, yet it gave light at night. Thus the one did not come near the other all night.

Then Moses stretched out his hand over the sea; and the Lord swept the sea back by a strong east wind all night and turned the sea into dry land, so the waters were divided. The sons of Israel went through the midst of the sea on the dry land, and the waters were like a wall to them on their right hand and on their left. Then the Egyptians took up the pursuit, and all Pharaoh's horses, his chariots and his horsemen went in after them into the midst of the sea. At the morning watch, the Lord looked down on the army of the Egyptians through the pillar of fire and cloud and brought the army of the Egyptians into confusion. He caused their chariot wheels to swerve, and He made them drive with difficulty; so the Egyptians said, "Let us flee from Israel, for the Lord is fighting for them against the Egyptians."

Then the Lord said to Moses, "Stretch out your hand over the sea so that the waters may come back over the Egyptians, over their chariots and their horsemen." So Moses stretched out his hand over the sea, and the sea returned to its normal state at daybreak, while the Egyptians were fleeing right into it; then the Lord overthrew the Egyptians in the midst of the sea. The waters returned and covered the chariots and the horsemen, even Pharaoh's entire army that had gone into the sea after them; not even one of them remained. But the sons of Israel walked on dry land through the midst of the sea, and the waters were like a wall to them on their right hand and on their left.

Thus the Lord saved Israel that day from the hand of the Egyptians, and Israel saw the Egyptians dead on the seashore. When Israel saw the great power which the Lord had used against the Egyptians, the people feared the Lord, and they believed in the Lord and in His servant Moses.

DAY 1 //providence

Then they said to Moses, "Is it because there were no graves in Egypt that you have taken us away to die in the wilderness? Why have you dealt with us in this way, bringing us out of Egypt? Is this not the word that we spoke to you in Egypt, saying, 'Leave us alone that we may serve the Egyptians'? For it would have been better for us to serve the Egyptians than to die in the wilderness." But Moses said to the people, "Do not fear! Stand by and see the salvation of the Lord which He will accomplish for you today; for the Egyptians whom you have seen today, you will never see them again forever. The Lord will fight for you while you keep silent." —Exodus 14: 11-14 (NASB)

The children of Israel were really struggling here. They'd gotten out of Egypt—finally left slavery behind—and I bet they were thinking their hard times were over. A little trek across the wilderness, and into the Promised Land they'd go. But instead there was obstacle after obstacle looming in front of them. Moses managed (through the **providence** of God) to steer them past the Philistines. But ahead of them there was the Red Sea. And behind them, coming in fast, was the whole Egyptian army. There were giants everywhere!

Are you there today? Seeing giants everywhere?

God, in his **providence**, always has a purpose for everything he allows in our lives. And there's nothing like giants to show us our own lack of ability, and our need for someone stronger to step in.

Here is the really fabulous thing about being in that place of powerlessness—it gets us seeing the truth. It's not up to us. It's up to God. And leaning on him is exactly where we should be all along.

So if you're feeling afraid today, lean into your Daddy's arms—the all-powerful Father who can conquer what you can't. The God in whom resides eternal hope, limitless power, and perfect healing. He says, "Do not fear. I will fight for you. Wait and see what's going to happen."

Dear Lord, you know my fearful heart. You know the weakness in the very core of me, the lack of ability to fix anything. Wrap your arms around me today. Help me breathe deep, and trust truly. Help me set all fear aside, to be still and know that you are in control and that your plan for my story is amazing. I pray all this in the precious name of Jesus. Amen

DAY 2 //providence

Then the Lord said to Moses, "Why are you crying out to Me? Tell the sons of Israel to go forward. As for you, lift up your staff and stretch out your hand over the sea and divide it, and the sons of Israel shall go through the midst of the sea on dry land. —Exodus 14: 15-16 (NASB)

I've always loved Psalm 119:105 which says, "*Your word is a lamp unto my feet and a light unto my path.*" It used to be that when I read that verse, I imagined something along the lines of a lighthouse beacon: Something that shines far into the distance, allowing you to chart your course. I know they didn't have those back in Bible times, but that's what I pictured.

Except awhile back I found out that when people smarter than me dissect that verse in the original language, they tell us that the word 'lamp' refers to a tiny little light, something more representative of a single candle. It's big enough to let you see only a step or two ahead of where you're going. You know, just enough that if you walk slowly and look sharp, you won't fall down the well. That's not remotely the thousand-candle illumination that I wish for when life gets complicated.

In hard times, I long to see far ahead—to recognize God's **providence** over all—and to know how this or that decision will look a decade from now. When God led Moses and the people out of Egypt, he didn't tell them all the details of the plan. But he did promise to watch over them. As they needed guidance, he led them step-by-step. So often that's what God does in my life too. He says, "For now, here's where I want you today. I'll tell you the next tiny move tomorrow. And have faith that I will take care of the next day, and the next, and the next."

Oh, that can be hard for us control-freak humans, can't it? With his grace and strength, we can do it. When we do release that longing to know, very often we will also discover that there's an unexpected peace that comes along with that release.

Because he's got this. He really does.

Dear Lord, in the middle of big and tough and scary decisions, light my way. Give me direction and wisdom and clarity in decision-making. But even more importantly, give me calm and faith when the way isn't so clear, when I can only see a step or two ahead. Help me remember that you really do have this covered. I pray all this in Jesus' name. Amen

DAY 3 //providence

The angel of God, who had been going before the camp of Israel, moved and went behind them; and the pillar of cloud moved from before them and stood behind them. So it came between the camp of Egypt and the camp of Israel; and there was the cloud along with the darkness, yet it gave light at night. Thus the one did not come near the other all night. (Verses 19-20 NASB)

So here the children of Israel were, stuck between the army of Egypt and a big body of water. They didn't know their next step, but night fell, and here's what God did for them. He gave them a shield and a night light all in one; a glowing wall of cloud between them and their enemy. They didn't know what was going to happen the next day. Have you ever stopped to consider that? We know the end of the story, the part that verifies God's **providence** above all else. The Israelites stood there staring at the water, knowing what was coming up behind them, without any knowledge of how they would get through it all. *But God knew.* As a part of his **providential** care of his people, he wanted to offer them rest.

Plenty of times when my life feels hard, I've called my momma to get her advice. Very often, along with other wise words, my momma will remind me to go to bed and sleep. "Things will look brighter in the morning," she always says.

Psalm 4:8 (HCSB) says, *"I will both lie down and sleep in peace, for you alone, oh LORD, make me live in safety."* When worry creeps in, it can be hard to remember that. God has our lives in his hands, we can sleep. We serve the God who holds the stars in place, a good and powerful God who promises to answer our every need at the right time. We can trust in him. We can rest.

*Dear Lord, We humans don't do so well at resting. Even when life is going well, we tend to want to be doing something. But especially when times are hard, it can be so tempting to worry and strive and agitate. And yet you call us to rest. Help me rest in you, to really abide, to see your hand of **providence** in my life, right there in the middle of the hard, in the middle of uncertainty. Give me the faith that lets me sleep like a baby in your all-powerful, all-comforting arms. I pray this in Jesus' name. Amen*

DAY 4 //providence

Then Moses stretched out his hand over the sea; and the Lord swept the sea back by a strong east wind all night and turned the sea into dry land, so the waters were divided. The sons of Israel went through the midst of the sea on the dry land, and the waters were like a wall to them on their right hand and on their left. —Exodus 14: 21-22 (NASB)

Can you imagine the moment when things begin to happen here? There the children of Israel were, on the edge of the Red Sea, with Pharaoh's men breathing down their necks. I bet more than a few of them were wishing God would make them a way just a little faster. I bet more than a few of them were wishing that through his **providence** he would rescue them, maybe even before that army had come into sight. Instead he waited.

Then, the miracle began to happen. That wind picked up and that sea began to get out of the way, and pretty soon they had a nice dry walking path, right across that Red Sea.

We all want to get to that place, don't we? The one where the path is clear and dry in front of us, and victory is imminent. Too often, God in his perfect wisdom lets us wait. Are you in that stage in your adoption journey? Absolutely certain that God is the one who needs to step in now, but not seeing any movement. At times like this, it can be really easy to be attacked by lies from Satan, can't it? Waiting is so hard.

I think it's because God's perfect timing rarely matches up with our ideas. When we don't see that sea getting out of the way, it can be all too easy to wonder if God has stopped working in our family's story.

Remember this truth: From eternity to eternity, God's **providential** timing has always been perfect. No matter how it feels, it won't stop being perfect for you and your family either. Even if you aren't seeing things happening, you can still trust he's there, working in a living and active way in your story. Don't be afraid to trust God's timing.

Dear Lord, you know how much I struggle with wanting things to be worked out now, for problems to be solved immediately. Help me trust your timing, your perfectly orchestrated plan for my life. Help me rest peacefully in you, even in the waiting. Amen.

DAY 5 //providence

Thus the Lord saved Israel that day from the hand of the Egyptians, and Israel saw the Egyptians dead on the seashore. When Israel saw the great power which the Lord had used against the Egyptians, the people feared the Lord, and they believed in the Lord and in His servant Moses. —Exodus 14:30-31 (NASB)

So often in our life, our troubles can look like giants standing there before us, immovable obstacles that stand in our path. In times like that, it's critically important to remember the size of the God we serve. He's not some small, weak thing, easily thwarted by humans or giants, for that matter.

We serve the God who created the universe, who made the sun and the moon and the stars, who allows every beat of our hearts. His plan for our lives will be accomplished no matter what seems to be standing in our way. Jeremiah 29:11 reminds us of his **providence**, *"For I know the plans I have for you, says the Lord, plans to prosper you and not to harm you, to give you a hope and a future."*

The detours, the painful paths we don't want to take, are the very places where he's planned for us to grow, to learn, to begin to trust more deeply in his **providence**.

You know in Genesis when Joseph was in Egypt, finally talking to his brothers about all the rotten stuff they'd done to him? He could have been mad. He had every right to be, but instead he saw God's **providence**, and he said, *"God sent me before you to preserve for you a remnant in the earth, and to keep you alive by a great deliverance."* (Genesis 45:7 NASB)

It is powerful to remind ourselves of that **providence**, because he didn't only do this for the children of Israel. He didn't only do this for Moses, and Joseph, and David, and Esther, and Peter, and Paul. He does it for us every day, whether we see that **providence** clearly or not. We serve a God who is always on time. A God whose perfect will cannot be thwarted. A God who can and does supply our every need.

Dear Heavenly Father, it can be so easy to feel overwhelmed by giants, by all the troubles and challenges in my life. Be with me, remind me of your power, your majesty, and your perfect Providence. Help me know down deep that you really are the answer to all my needs, the soother of all my worries, the true and best Lover of my soul. Thank you so much for your perfect work in my life and in the story of my family. Amen

his presence

Throughout the adoption process—and throughout much of our lives—it is common to wonder, "Where are you, God?" The waiting, delays, disappointments, and frustrations can leave you feeling hopeless and afraid. This week, **RACHEL HARRISON** walks us through Elijah's story of hopelessness and fear. Even though he had just witnessed God win a big victory, the trials overwhelmed Elijah and he was ready to give up. As Rachel reminds us, God was present, even when Elijah lost hope. It is **his presence** that sustains us and nourishes us, no matter the situation.

SCRIPTURE FOCUS /// I KINGS 19:1-18 (ESV)

Ahab told Jezebel all that Elijah had done, and how he had killed all the prophets with the sword. Then Jezebel sent a messenger to Elijah, saying, "So may the gods do to me and more also, if I do not make your life as the life of one of them by this time tomorrow." Then he was afraid, and he arose and ran for his life and came to Beersheba, which belongs to Judah, and left his servant there.

But he himself went a day's journey into the wilderness and came and sat down under a broom tree. And he asked that he might die, saying, "It is enough; now, O Lord, take away my life, for I am no better than my fathers." And he lay down and slept under a broom tree. And behold, an angel touched him and said to him, "Arise and eat." And he looked, and behold, there was at his head a cake baked on hot stones and a jar of water. And he ate and drank and lay down again.

And the angel of the Lord came again a second time and touched him and said, "Arise and eat, for the journey is too great for you." And he arose and ate and drank, and went in the strength of that food forty days and forty nights to Horeb, the mount of God. There he came to a cave and lodged in it.

And behold, the word of the Lord came to him and he said to him, "What are you doing here, Elijah?" He said, "I have been very jealous for the Lord, the God of hosts. For the people of Israel have forsaken your covenant, thrown down your altars, and killed your prophets with the sword, and I, even I only, am left, and they seek my life, to take it away."

And he said, "Go out and stand on the mount before the Lord." And behold, the Lord passed by, and a great and strong wind tore the mountains and broke in pieces the rocks before the Lord, but the Lord was not in the wind. And after the wind an earthquake, but the Lord was not in the earthquake. And after the earthquake a fire, but the Lord was not in the fire. And after the fire, the sound of a low whisper. And when Elijah heard it, he wrapped his face in his cloak and went out and stood at the entrance of the cave. And behold, there came a voice to him and said, "What are you doing here, Elijah?"

He said, "I have been very jealous for the Lord, the God of hosts. For the people of Israel have forsaken your covenant, thrown down your altars, and killed your prophets with the sword, and I, even I only, am left and they seek my life, to take it away."

And the Lord said to him, "Go, return on your way to the wilderness of Damascus. And when you arrive, you shall anoint Hazael to be king over Syria. And Jehu the son of Nimshi you shall anoint to be king over Israel, and Elisha the son of Shaphat of Abel-meholoah you shall anoint to be prophet in your place. "And the one who escapes from the sword of Hazael shall Jehu put to death, and the one who escapes from the sword of Jehu shall Elisha put to death. "Yet I will leave seven thousand in Israel, all the knees that have not bowed to Baal, and every mouth that has not kissed him." (NKJV)

DAY 1 *His presence*

For our family, the process of adoption the first time around was long and full of challenges. There were disappointments, setbacks and wondering if it would ever happen. And then, it did! The day I met my son was nerve wracking and magical, all at the same time. It was love at first sight for me and the bonding started immediately. As things progressed, the adoption finalized and I felt so fulfilled, finally having my son in my arms.

I thought that was it.

But that was just the beginning. From my view, God had moved in amazing ways to put this particular child in my arms and I stood in awe of the miracle. But then there was more. Literally, the day after our adoption finalized, the trials began. It started with pneumonia, which turned into a fever for five months that all of the medical specialists at Johns Hopkins could not diagnose. We literally went from one to the next: Infectious disease, immunology, rheumatology. Each one had tests and questions, and everyone wanted to know a more detailed genetic history than we were able to provide.

In my spirit, I thought, "This does not seem right!" I was engaged, trying to help my child and trying to find the answers, but I felt very discouraged. In my assessment, my son had already come from a hard place and my husband and I had waited years and years for this moment... and now this? I was not prepared for the ongoing trials of this journey.

I felt much like Elijah in I Kings 19:1-18. Just before this passage, Elijah challenges the prophets of Baal to a dual: *whose God will bring fire?* Of course, God wins, the prophets of Baal are put to death, and it is a victorious day. And then the bottom falls out for Elijah, too. Jezebel sends word that she intends to kill him for putting to death the prophets of Baal. Elijah becomes overwhelmed by this threat. He seeks isolation, he feels hopeless, and the memory of God's victory seems to fade away.

But in Elijah's desolation, and despite Elijah's forgetfulness of the past victory, God provides nourishment for Elijah. I Kings 19:5-6 (NIV) tells us, *"Then [Elijah] lay down under the bush and fell asleep. All at once an angel touched him and said, 'Get up and eat.' He looked around, and there by his head was some bread baked over hot coals, and a jar of water. He ate and drank and then lay down again."*

As each challenge continues to rise, God somehow reminds me through a friend, a moment with him or just through seeing his provision, that he is *Present*. And it is **his presence** that sustains me.

*Lord, help me to remember that your **presence** is always with me, to sustain and nourish me, no matter what the journey entails.*

DAY 2 //his presence

In the story of Elijah, it says that God continued to provide food and drink and rest for Elijah for forty days and forty nights (I Kings 19:8). It seems that God was in no hurry. Moreover, he knew how long Elijah needed to rejuvenate and overcome his fear.

As I reflect upon God's patience, I wish that I had more of his perspective. I am often in a hurry to see things work out and to find a solution. I experienced the challenge of waiting when we approached adoption the second time around.

Eventually I overcame the shock of the medical issues, things resolved and returned to normal. My husband and I felt called to adopt again, so we set about the process of adoption once more. This time, all of the paperwork was easier to handle, and the timing of the process was understandable. We were thrilled to learn that instead of waiting for three years, this time there was the possibility of a child at the time of our home study. Again, I became very excited at the victory. This seemed like a great blessing to have another child and not have all the heartache of the wait.

Although everything seemed to be in place, I started to wonder as our birthmother's due date approached. I began to hear nothing. Everything got quiet. The adoption agency had not heard anything either. We had met, had signed agreements, made plans... The silence was almost more than I could bear. At times I would convince myself it was fine, nothing to worry about. And at other times, the worst-case scenario would hit hard. The due date came and went with no word. About a week later, we got a call from the adoption agency stating that the birth mom had changed her mind.

Thud.

Here I was again. After a great move of God, I again felt the weight of disappointment. I had questions, I had emotional attachment to this child, and I needed to just wait, to grieve.

I learned in that process that by allowing myself to grieve this loss, I was slowly opening my heart up for something new, for the next thing that God had for me.

So, I stopped and just grieved.

God's presence was with me and the healing came. It wasn't the same forty days that Elijah needed, but I learned that God will wait for me to go through my own process. Whether it is grieving or resting, he knows our limitations. He will wait until we are ready.

Lord, help me to embrace the process of adoption and all the emotions that come with it. Thank you for your patience and sustenance.

DAY 3 *His presence*

People ask me all the time about my experiences with adoption. Many are considering it themselves, and my standard response is that adoption is a wonderful, amazing journey, *but* it is not for the faint of heart.

You see, my experience continues with the ups and downs of the adoption journey. Not long after the dissolution of a hoped-for adoption, we were matched with another birth mother. Within a few days, my second beautiful son was born! Again, this was such a monumental blessing. We were now a family of four, and things progressed smoothly as we all adjusted and attached to our newest family member.

It was the calm before the storm.

As we started to get a handle on some of the issues and challenges facing my older son, my youngest began to have challenges of his own. It came on suddenly and at a time when I could barely keep up with the waves that kept coming toward me. Another surprise issue, another set of unknowns. I found myself at the point of discouragement again, only this time I didn't know if I could handle any more.

In seeking God, this story of Elijah continued to resonate with me: *"And he said, 'Go out and stand on the mount before the Lord.' And behold, the Lord passed by, and a great and strong wind tore the mountains and broke in pieces the rocks before the Lord, but the Lord was not in the wind. And after the wind, an earthquake, but the Lord was not in the earthquake. And after the earthquake a fire, but the Lord was not in the fire. And after the fire, the sound of a low whisper."* (1 Kings 19:11-12).

God demonstrated his power to Elijah in these verses, but also chose to meet him in a quiet whisper. I think Elijah was looking for something big. After all, he had experienced big moves of God before. Instead, God simply wanted to communicate with him... to remind him of **his presence**. *Quietly.* Perhaps when he least expected it.

Having two children with special needs has shifted from a big storm of shock waves in my life to a daily learning process of how to meet needs differently and how to find God in the big and in the small. I find his presence and his guidance in still, small moments. In these, I am strengthened for the journey ahead. No matter what it brings.

*Lord, help me be still. Remind me that you find me here and that your **presence** is always with me.*

DAY 4 //his presence

As we follow Elijah in this story, God patiently repeats the same question he asked earlier: "*What are you doing here, Elijah?*" (1 Kings 19:13b). He so gently inquires of Elijah again, but the fact that he asks a second time shows his power, **presence**, and desire to communicate with him. Sadly, Elijah answers the question the same way he did before.

His answer is all about being afraid, focusing on the people who seek to kill him, "*I have been very jealous for the Lord, the God of hosts. For the people of Israel have forsaken your covenant, thrown down your altars, and killed your prophets with the sword, and I, even I only, am left and they seek my life, to take it away.*" (verse 14) Poor Elijah is just as destitute as he was at the beginning of this passage.

It makes me feel better to know that Elijah was prone to repeat conversations and repeat lessons to learn with God! In the ups and downs of the adoption journey, I kept coming back, over and over again to ask, "Why God?" I may not be finished asking that question, but something did come along to shift my thinking.

It came in a book, a group study written specifically for adoptive moms by my friend, Paula Freeman (*A Place I Didn't Belong*). In the process of going through this book and reading the words of another adoptive mom, I recognized a very simple, but very profound truth: *Love is not enough.* That may sound shocking, but it is true. Believing that love was enough to help our family and to help my children was keeping me from some realities of assessing their needs.

Don't get me wrong, love is a necessary ingredient in all families and certainly in adoption. It is a beautiful notion to give love to a child who needs a family. Although love is essential, it cannot provide the therapeutic interventions often necessary to help children from hard places.

As I allowed myself to experience **God's presence**, he opened up new ideas and concepts that gave me direction, discernment and wisdom. In his time, I was able to see things differently and to understand that there was a plan moving forward. My perspective shifted, thanks to the insight, and I was able to recognize a path toward greater healing and wholeness.

In the same way, God told Elijah to "*Go, return on your way to the wilderness of Damascus.*" He laid out a plan for Elijah and helped him take action again.

Lord, help me listen to you as you speak to me. Give me your direction when I am not able to see a clear path.

DAY 5 *His presence*

The journey of adoption can be isolating. There are challenges and situations that are very different than those experienced in the typical parenting scenario. Things like loss, race, grief, and identity are all more complex for adoptees and for adoptive parents. When surrounded by families who are not dealing with these complexities, I can begin to feel like I am alone in the challenges that I face.

The same was true for Elijah. He said, "...and I, *even I only,* am left..." (1 Kings 19:14). He hibernated out in the wilderness for forty days and nights, with nothing but some nourishment and a couple of brief conversations with God. He believed that all of Israel had deserted God. He believed he alone was left as the sole believer in God and that his life was in peril.

No wonder he lost hope.

Yet, God speaks at the end of the passage declares, "*Yet I will leave seven thousand in Israel, all the knees that have not bowed to Baal, and every mouth that has not kissed him.*" (1 Kings 19:18). So Elijah learned the reality: he believed he alone remained as a follower of God, when in fact, there were seven thousand believers left in Israel who remained true to God! What a big discrepancy between his perspective and the accurate picture: Elijah is no longer alone and God had raised up other leaders.

When I look at the world from my vantage point, so often it is only a microcosm of what truly exists. God alone can see the big picture, from the beginning to the end, and the way that everything fits together. In fact, of all the children in the entire world, he placed *just these two* in my home. It was truly a miracle of time and place that I am the mother of these children. How quickly I forget that truth in the face of challenge and struggle.

God revealed many other believers to Elijah, letting him know that he was not alone. I have also discovered a great community of other moms who can talk openly about the joys and challenges of adoption. Knowing there are many adoptive moms out there struggling through all the different parts of this journey creates a sense of strength in me. I believe that God desires us to know that we are not alone and that there is a community that can support us, whatever the challenges.

It is **his presence** that often reaches us as we experience the presence of others who can support us and understand the journey.

I want to remind every adoptive mom out there, *you are not alone*! This is a tough journey, but one that can be shared. In sharing openly and connecting with other adoptive moms, you will have the support you need for the journey ahead.

*Lord, show us your **presence**. In your mercy lead us to others who can share in our joys and challenges as adoptive moms.*

his faithfulness

Sometimes it doesn't seem like God is in control. Things appear out of our control, whether it is infertility, waiting for referrals, or working through attachment and bonding challenges with a newly adopted child, but God is **faithful** through it all. He sees the bigger picture and orchestrates things in only ways that he can. This week **LISA WILLIAMS** shares what God taught her about his **faithfulness**, during her adoption process. She takes us through the story of Joseph to see how God was **faithful** despite what seemed like devastating circumstances.

SCRIPTURE FOCUS //GENESIS 37, 39-41

So when Joseph came to his brothers, they stripped him of his robe—the ornate robe he was wearing— and they took him and threw him into the cistern. The cistern was empty; there was no water in it. As they sat down to eat their meal, they looked up and saw a caravan of Ishmaelites coming from Gilead. Their camels were loaded with spices, balm and myrrh, and they were on their way to take them down to Egypt. Judah said to his brothers, "What will we gain if we kill our brother and cover up his blood? Come, let's sell him to the Ishmaelites and not lay our hands on him; after all, he is our brother, our own flesh and blood." His brothers agreed. So when the Midianite merchants came by, his brothers pulled Joseph up out of the cistern and sold him for twenty shekels of silver to the Ishmaelites, who took him to Egypt. (Genesis 37:23-28 NIV)

Now Joseph had been taken down to Egypt. Potiphar, an Egyptian who was one of Pharaoh's officials, the captain of the guard, bought him from the Ishmaelites who had taken him there. The Lord was with Joseph so that he prospered, and he lived in the house of his Egyptian master. When his master saw that the Lord was with him and that the Lord gave him success in everything he did, Joseph found favor in his eyes and became his attendant. Potiphar put him in charge of his household, and he entrusted to his care everything he owned, and after a while his master's wife took notice of Joseph and said, "Come to bed with me!" But he refused. "With me in charge," he told her, "my master does not concern himself with anything in the house; everything he owns he has entrusted to my care.

One day he went into the house to attend to his duties, and none of the household servants was inside. She caught him by his cloak and said, "Come to bed with me!" But he left his cloak in her hand and ran out of the house.

Joseph's master took him and put him in prison, the place where the king's prisoners were confined. But while Joseph was there in the prison, the Lord was with him; he showed him kindness and granted him favor in the eyes of the prison warden. (Genesis 39:1-4, 7-8, 11-12, 20-21 NIV)

So Pharaoh said to Joseph, "I hereby put you in charge of the whole land of Egypt." Then Pharaoh took his signet ring from his finger and put it on Joseph's finger. He dressed him in robes of fine linen and put a gold chain around his neck. He had him ride in a chariot as his second-in-command, and people shouted before him, "Make way!" Then he put him in charge of the whole land of Egypt. (Genesis 41:41-43 NIV)

DAY 1 *His faithfulness*

Life often catches us off guard. Joseph went to the fields to fetch his brothers, completely oblivious to the fact that he was about to be thrown into a cistern, or a pit. He was simply doing what his father asked. But Joseph's father loved him more than his other brothers. His brothers were already jealous of him when Joseph had two dreams indicating that his brothers would bow down to him. That certainly didn't help matters. When the brothers saw him coming, they plotted to kill him, and that is how we find Joseph in a pit.

Infertility caught my husband and me off guard. We had a plan. It did not go as expected (and now we're so thankful!) and we were in a "pit."

We all end up in a pit eventually. A pit can be any number of things, including infertility, adoption loss, financial struggles, difficulty bonding with a newly adopted child. It is critical to remember that the pits we fall into are temporary. Pits are not fun! That is why they are called the pits! But oh, can you learn from them!

Have you heard the song "Heal the Wound" by Point of Grace? The chorus reads:

> Heal the wound but leave the scar
> A reminder of how merciful you are
> I am broken, torn apart
> Take the pieces of this heart
> And heal the wound but leave the scar

Same idea. God can use the pits in this life for our ultimate good and for his glory. Pits are places of temporary pressure. It is in those pits that we really learn to trust him, knowing that he is ultimately **faithful**. It's easy to trust him when everything is going well. But in the pit? It is so much harder! Especially when you don't know how it will all play out! That is why we call it faith.

Think of how many people in the Bible encountered pits. Hannah was in the pit of infertility (1 Samuel 1). Job lost loved ones, health, and pretty much everything else (Job). Christ was even in a pit when Satan led him into the wilderness (Matthew 4:1-11). God allowed all of those pits and will allow them in our lives, too. Remember, nothing will happen to you that does not first pass through the hands of God.

I don't know about you, but I want God to "heal the wounds but leave the scars."

Dear God, I can't see my way out of this pit, but I know you can. I can only see the here and now. Lord please "heal the wound but leave the scar."

DAY 2 // *His faithfulness*

We left off with Joseph in a pit. His brothers saw the Ishmaelites coming and decided to pull Joseph out of the pit and sell him. He was taken to Egypt, where he was sold to Potiphar, the captain of the guard. Meanwhile, Jacob was led to believe a wild animal ate his son.

The Lord was with Joseph in everything he did. Potiphar took notice and put Joseph in charge of everything he owned. Potiphar's wife was attracted to Joseph and tried over and over to get him into bed with her. Joseph refused repeatedly.

One day there was no one else in the house and she came on to him once again. This time, she grabbed him by the cloak. He ran away. This is a story for another day, but sometimes we just need to run from temptation. He left his cloak in her hands. She made up a story about Joseph trying to rape her, and when Potiphar found out, he threw Joseph in prison.

In prison? *That's not fair!* Have you ever thought that? That life wasn't fair? You have probably heard "well, life ISN'T fair." God never promises us that life will be easy, but he does promise that he'll be **faithful** and that he'll never leave us.

When we found no heartbeat at 14 weeks in our pregnancy, my world crumbled. I never questioned God, but I did have a lot of questions *for* him. It wasn't fair. We had prayed so much for this child! We had gone through many infertility treatments! Later, while in the thick of the adoption process, we found out that Russia was requiring a third trip. That meant more time for my child to be in the orphanage. Why?! Then I received the following email:

"I have to say the only reason I can surmise [for all of the hurting, pain, etc.] is to point a finger at one person and one person only. It would stand to reason that this one person would be the only one who would benefit from any resistance to a child being placed in a loving home or a Christian couple uniting with the child God intended to be a part of their family, because he is the only person who would want this process to be extended, if not all together stopped. Yep, you guessed it, Satan. While it seems our struggle is with earthly things, it is really a spiritual battle. You are at war. And, not only that, you are winning. Therefore, it stands to reason the attacks would increase. But, my dear friend, you know the end. You know God is victorious! He defeats Satan. Hold fast to his plan. Don't lose sight of it, no matter what! Tighten your belt, devote even more time to God's word, prayer and hold on tight to Jesus' hand."

Amen!

*Dear Heavenly Father, help me to hold fast when life throws me curve balls knowing that in the end you are **faithful** and you win.*

DAY 3 *His faithfulness*

Today we pick up with spiritual warfare. *"For our struggle is not against flesh and blood, but against the rulers, against the authorities, against the powers of this dark world and against the spiritual forces of evil in the heavenly realms."* (Ephesians 6:12) The battles we face in order to bring our kids home and bond with them is not against the country, it's not against our agency, or anyone/anything that might stand in the way. It's against Satan! And the good thing is that we know how it ends!

To get our son home was a battle. Russia required three trips at the time.

We missed my only brother's wedding to go on the first trip and my husband was right in the middle of a huge multi-week licensing exam process at work. Then, there was not being able to find our contact person when we landed in Moscow. This was ok, since we are fluent in Russian... NOT! This somehow put us "in breech of our contract," making the whole process a risk.

On a Friday afternoon in our first trip, we had to get our official referral acceptance notarized. We were playing with our son, with our facilitator, when our translator called frantically to let us know that since it was a holiday weekend, the notary office would be closing early. We dropped everything, took our son back to his room, and met our translator on our way. We got to the notary office with only about 10 minutes before they closed.

There was a five-month wait between the first and second trips. I had to get fingerprinted no less then seven times. We had to update our home study. Then, I had my stroke the day after we returned home from our second trip, once again putting the whole process in jeopardy. I could go on and on, and I'm sure you have your own stories, too.

Remember, the devil does not want these children in a loving home. Especially not into a home that loves the Lord. The enemy tries to discourage us. *"The thief comes only to steal and kill and destroy; I have come that they may have life, and have it to the full."* (John 10:10 NIV)

God can, and will, take all that Satan meant for evil and use it for his ultimate glory. He IS **faithful**, we just have to trust him in the details.

Lord, help me stand firm when the devil attacks. Help me put on the full armor of God: "with the belt of truth buckled around your waist, with the breastplate of righteousness in place, and with your feet fitted with the readiness that comes from the gospel of peace. In addition to all this, take up the shield of faith, with which you can extinguish all the flaming arrows of the evil one. Take the helmet of salvation and the sword of the Spirit, which is the word of God." (Ephesians 6:14-17 NIV)

DAY 4 //his faithfulness

Trusting God in the details is not easy. I'm sure Joseph wonders why he was in the pit of prison. I sure wondered about my pit.

My husband and I experienced infertility for years. We were pregnant twice and both pregnancies ended in miscarriages. With the second one, we had finally allowed ourselves to let our guard down, tell people, plan for the future, etc., when it happened. I felt the baby move for the first time on a Monday night and on Tuesday morning, at a routine visit, we discovered that our baby did not have a heartbeat. We were absolutely devastated.

Fast-forward to after much prayer when we were on our first adoption trip to Russia. We were at the orphanage, meeting with the social worker. She was showing us all of our son's paperwork, and when she turned around the birth certificate I started to sob. His birthday is the exact day of our due date, and not just the date, but the same year. Wow! If that doesn't scream, "God is in the details," I don't know what does.

What the devil intended for harm, God used for our good. "*And we know that in all things God works for the good of those who love him, who have been called according to his purpose.*" (Romans 8:28 NIV) Sometimes we see it this side of Heaven, sometimes we don't. It makes me think of the song "Blessings" by Laura Story. The chorus goes:

'Cause what if your blessings come through rain drops
What if your healing comes through tears
What if a thousand sleepless nights are what it takes to know you're near
What if trials of this life are your mercies in disguise

Blessings are not always rainbows and sunshine. I once heard that a blessing can be anything that makes you cry out to God. It's probably a different way for you to look at the pits and trials of life. While we were going through infertility, loss, and adoption drama, we weren't thinking of it as a blessing. But look what it brought us... a beautiful boy who was always intended for our family.

Our merciful and eternally **faithful** God can see the bigger picture. Just trust in the ups and downs that he sees it all.

Father, I want to see life's trials as you do. I want to count everything that makes me call out to you as a blessing. Help me trust your ways.

DAY 5 //his faithfulness

God does see the bigger picture. Caleb Chapman (Christian artist Steven Curtis Chapman's son) describes it as a tapestry. On the back, up close, all you see is the ugly knots. Farther back, on the front, you see the beautiful, full picture. I've also heard it described like a cake. Individually the ingredients, flour, raw eggs, are gross, but when put together they make a yummy cake. Individually, the pits and trials of this life, the knots or ingredients, don't make sense. But God can see the completed tapestry. He knows that the cake will turn out. We just have to trust that he'll be faithful with the ingredients.

Let's take one last look at Joseph's story. We left him in prison where the Lord was with him (he is always with us!) and the warden put him in charge of everything there. In the prison were the king's cup bearer and chief baker, for they had offended the king. They both had dreams and Joseph, through the Lord, correctly interpreted the dreams.

Some time later, Pharaoh, the new king, has a dream. The cup bearer, who has been released from prison, finally remembers Joseph, who is fetched from prison and once again Joseph (the Lord really) interprets a dream. Pharaoh is so pleased that, upon Joseph's suggestion, he makes Joseph the second in command. In charge of all of Egypt! Joseph, with the help of the Lord, Pharaoh's dream, and prior planning, goes on to feed people from across the world!

Once again, God saw the whole picture. He used the pit, bondage, and prison to save all of Egypt, which also provided a way for the Israelites to survive, even though Egypt would prove to be full of its own "pits" for God's people. Wow! God used our struggles to bring us our son, and I look forward to see how he'll use my stroke and all its struggles for his glory.

Since music speaks to me so much I wanted to leave you with lyrics from "**Faithful**" by Steven Curtis Chapman.

You are faithful!
You are faithful!
When you give and when you take away,
Even then still your name is faithful!
You are faithful!
And with everything inside of me,
I am choosing to believe
You are faithful

*God, you're **faithful**. I choose today to trust that you see the completed picture, the whole tapestry. Thank you for your **faithfulness**.*

my shepherd

Precious children. We have become precious children in the family of our Heavenly Father. The concept of adoption and God's example of grafting in strangers and making them family is a theme that permeates the Old and New Testament. Adoption in the literal sense is also a great picture of Christ-like love made tangible.

What a gift, that our Father works in such concrete, relatable themes, so that we might understand the great depth of his heart toward us. How important to us adoptive and foster mamas, neck deep in the daily challenges, are these beautiful images of our own adoption into God's family.

Ezekiel, a book often overlooked in our quiet times, is packed full of amazing images of the sacrificial love of God for his people. As mamas with our own flocks, we may soak in encouragement from the rich passage of Ezekiel 34: 11-16. This week, **WENDY LANKFORD** helps us examine our God as he is pictured as the seeker, provider, **shepherd**, healer/rescuer, and protector.

SCRIPTURE FOCUS //EZEKIEL 34: 11-16 (ESV)

For thus says the Lord God: Behold, I, I myself will search for my sheep and will seek them out. As a shepherd seeks out his flock when he is among his sheep that have been scattered, so will I seek out my sheep, and I will rescue them from all places where they have been scattered on a day of clouds and thick darkness. And I will bring them out from the peoples and gather them from the countries, and will bring them into their own land. And I will feed them on the mountains of Israel, by the ravines, and in all the inhabited places of the country. I will feed them with good pasture, and on the mountain heights of Israel shall be their grazing land. There they shall lie down in good grazing land, and on rich pasture they shall feed on the mountains of Israel. I myself will be the shepherd of my sheep, and I myself will make them lie down, declares the Lord God. I will seek the lost, and I will bring back the strayed, and I will bind up the injured, and I will strengthen the weak, and the fat and the strong I will destroy. I will feed them in justice.

DAY 1 //my shepherd

My heart raced. My tongue felt thick. My eyes darted and scanned the neighborhood. I called his name again in my loudest voice, ignoring the stares of annoyed neighbors. I felt sick and dizzy. Where could he be? I had taken my eyes away from the quiet court for just a minute to grab a glass of water while my seemingly occupied five-year-old played on the common area in front of my house. At that moment, I would have done anything to find my little boy. My precious one was lost, and what relief I experienced when his dirty precocious self popped out from behind a neighbor's house. I scooped him up in my arms and held him tight.

In the adoption world, there is a similar phenomenon, when prospective parents begin the quest to add precious ones to their fold. There is a frantic activity that goes along with the process. Our motivations and desires may vary, but somewhere in the heart of our quest is finding a child that is vulnerable, and in need of care, and bringing him into our hearts and homes.

Behold, I, I myself will search for my sheep and will seek them out. (v.11) We don't serve a God who wound a clock and watched it tick at a distance. We serve a God who lived among us, in the dirt and the discomfort that came with the maligned job of **shepherd**.

As a shepherd seeks out his flock when he is among his sheep that have been scattered, so will I seek out my sheep, and I will rescue them from all places where they have been scattered on a day of clouds and thick darkness.

In the quiet and desolation of the wilderness, those sheep were not just a precious commodity to the **shepherd** of Biblical times, but treasured creatures with whom he developed an intimate relationship. He knew their personalities, their distinguishing marks, and their habits. He knew those who were prone to wander and those who remained close. What is so substantial about this picture of God as **shepherd** is that the same God, who created the sheep in the beginning, is among his sheep, seeking them out. They have always belonged to him, but now he goes to all of the places where they may be scattered, to find each one and unite them to the flock. What a perfect picture of the imperfect love we have for the sheep in our family's fold.

*Father God, you are the great **Shepherd**. You are ever leading, guiding, correcting, and redeeming your little lambs. Give us a shepherd's heart, a heart that seeks and finds lost children, a heart able to see through the mess and look into the hearts of these little ones, even if it is difficult and costly. We know you will lead us and we will follow. You know our names and we belong to you. Amen.*

DAY 2 //my shepherd

We got a call on a Friday with exciting news. There was a little boy, recently born with Down Syndrome, that needed a family. "Get a bucket of chicken and we'll celebrate," my brash and optimistic husband said. Across Maryland there was a little helpless boy, who could now be my child. A boy I had never met, never touched, never seen a picture of. Yet somehow mine.

We needed to respond to the agency by Monday, but the answer was already clear to us. We would soon have a tiny son, with Albanian birth parents, heart defects, and Down Syndrome. I like categories and boxes and clearly defined outcomes. But we were blazing a new trail that was terrifying. What would Down syndrome and congenital heart defects look like? I didn't even know where Albania was! (All I could imagine were the tracksuit clad gangsters in some Liam Neeson action thriller.)

I was reminded of God's covenant promise to his people. He would be their God and they would be his people. This little boy was not defined by his nationality, or by his diagnosis.

I'm not diminishing the fact that many of our children may come from lands far away, or from cultures foreign to us. I'm not saying that their heritage isn't part of who they are, but they are not defined by what has happened to them or where they come from; instead, they are defined by the family they are a part of. He would now be one of my own, my little sheep to **shepherd**.

"And I will bring them out from the peoples and gather them from the countries, and will bring them into their own land." (Verse 13)

When we look around, we may see little diversity of race or culture. Some of our kids may be the only "foreigner" other children have met. They may be the first person with a wheelchair, a cleft lip, a tattoo, or slang-laden speech that those around us have ever encountered. But this is no mistake, or second class distinction. These children have been sought by God, just as we have been grafted into God's chosen people.

There are no accidents.

Not only does he seek his sheep, but he *"brings them into their own land."* It doesn't say he brings them into a new land, or a strange land, but "their own land," implying it is a heritage that may be new and strange, but a land that has always been theirs. Similarly, our adopted children, through less than ideal circumstances, enter into our fold to be raised in "the nurture and admonition of the Lord." That is the greatest provision we could ever receive or ever hope to share with our kids.

Lord, help me to embrace this great heritage you have so graciously bestowed on me, a former stranger and alien. I am your daughter, help me to live in that reality and help me to reflect it to my children.

DAY 3 //my shepherd

Perilous. Sweltering. Cold. Filthy. The terrain of the nomadic shepherding life is not for the faint of heart. The **shepherd** must know the territory, he must know where to find the good grazing lands, where the fresh water is, where the obstacles and dangers are for his flock. Sheep are weak, and often find themselves helpless and in danger. A **shepherd** must know his sheep. He smells like sheep, he sleeps among the sheep, he eats, breathes, and thinks sheep. It is a thankless job, a wearying, sacrificial, without-a-day-off sort of job.

Sound familiar?

On those days when you are not sure how many days it has been since you've had a shower, when you count goldfish and chocolate milk as a complete meal, when you can't wait until your husband gets home to tag out, this passage can be an encouragement. Parenting is hard. Parenting kids from hard places can be even harder, but we are not solitary **shepherds.** We have the creator of the sheep as our Guide.

"There they shall lie down in good grazing land, and on rich pasture they shall feed on the mountains of Israel." (Verse 14)

We are helpless and weak, but the Lord is gracious and when we feed on him, when we drink from the living water, we can rest in his protection and love. He is leading us through the highs and the lows so that we may grow to be more like our Master.

Sometimes a shepherd must make his sheep lie down. As Phillip Keller tells us, in his book, *A Shepherd Looks at Psalm 23*, "The strange thing about sheep is that because of their very make-up, it is almost impossible for them to be made to lie down unless four requirements are met. Owing to their timidity they refuse to lie down unless they are free of all fear. Because of the social behavior within a flock, sheep will not lie down unless they are free from friction with others of their kind. If tormented by flies or parasites, sheep will not lie down. Only when free of these pests can they relax. Lastly, sheep will not lie down as long as they feel in need of finding food. They must be free from hunger."

He is walking alongside us when we stumble and are wandering. Isn't that the same role that we take with our children? We walk through the valleys and fight their battles alongside them. We dry tears, and calm rages, and pick up the pieces with them. We meet their needs with good things, we show them the richness of the Gospel.

Lord Jesus, Thank you for making us lie down. You meet our fear with comfort, you place us in families, you show us our sin and you change us. Help us to seek you when we feel weak and unable to navigate the hills and valleys with our children. Help us to rest in your care.

DAY 4 //my shepherd

Most of the time he held it together. He was polite, helpful, and thoughtful. Now he was a little drunk, and weeping openly. "I'm in so much pain. I've lost so many people." The names of some of his losses are inked on his skin. *He has longed to belong as far back as he can remember.*

As he vacillated between deep sorrow and anger, I wanted to pull him close, stroke his hair, and whisper, just like I had done with my other babies, "Shhhh, Mommy's here." But I'm not his mommy.

But then, just like with my other children, I'm done for, he's mine, there's no going back. This boy has been through lifetimes of pain in his 21 years. He came without hope, out of money, with no more couches to surf.

He was one of the lost boys, a former foster kid without a happy ending. At age eight, he started down a path of more foster placements than I can count on my hands. His parents and brother are dead. His file is full of labels. He listens to loud rap music and uses words that would make my Grandma blush. He lives waiting for the next family to tell him he's not welcome.

"I will seek the lost..." (from Verse 16)

If you strip away the tough ghetto-gangsta-persona he sometimes puts on out of habit, you would see one of the most tender, sensitive young men. *In the world's eyes, he's a lost cause.* When he first came to meet us, I felt the same way. I just figured he was another one of my husband's fixer-uppers.

"...and I will bring back the strayed,"

God has given me new eyes, though. He's not a lost cause, he was a lost boy, but now he is found. He is damaged goods, but before Christ, so were we. God sought us, rescued us, healed us. He didn't see us as the sum of our circumstances, but as a precious lamb in need of care.

"I will bind up the injured..."

Many of our kids have invisible wounds, hidden under years of defense mechanisms and masks. Just as injured animals fight and claw and howl, we may have days of dealing with past hurts and old patterns.

But take heart, mama. You can't heal, rescue and restore. Only our Savior can. You can live like your **Shepherd**, though. You can slog through the mud and wind to pull your sheep back from the precipice. You can grow callouses praying for your little (and big) lambs. You can witness the amazing healing power of your **shepherd** as he cares for those most precious to you.

Holy Spirit, guide and direct me as I seek to love and point my child to the healing only you can bring. Thank you for doing the work and allowing us to witness your power in the lives of our families. May the lives of our children give you great Glory.

DAY 5 //my shepherd

"I will strengthen the weak, and the fat and the strong I will destroy. I will feed them in justice." (v.16) My mind couldn't reconcile the pictures I was seeing. Skin stretched like sallow latex over a ghastly skeleton. She was dressed in an ill-fitting, soiled outfit. At nine, weighing a mere 20 lbs, she stared lifelessly through the bars of the crib that held her captive. Tears poured down my face as I wept over the lost years of that little girl and with joy over the family full of loving arms to wrap around her.

How do things like this happen? How can life be so devalued? We have seen the hard places, and the injustices that our children have endured. There may be no earthly justice. Sin has spoiled paradise, but take heart, **shepherd**. *There will be no lost sheep.* God will find them all and, in the end, he will hand out justice to those who fed themselves instead of his sheep.

What do we do in the meantime? How do we wait for Jesus' justice and still be obedient in the waiting? First, we must be fed. We must stay close to our **shepherd**. Because we are emptied so often, we need to make that precious time to be quiet and to be filled with God's Word preached, prayer, and fellowship with him and his people. *Dear sisters, find a church body where you can be filled and embraced.*

We must also take this calling of mothering the lost sheep very seriously. These sheep are precious to him. We must lay down our own lives for the sheep he has given us. Our kids don't come with instruction manuals; each one is gloriously and fearfully different from the next. *Know your sheep and pray for wisdom to love and guide them in a way that points them to Christ and the hope of the Gospel.*

And we must help one another as a tribe. When our sisters are hurting, we need to step in and fill the gaps. Others may not understand the issues we face, and we need to bolster and love one another through the good and difficult days. We serve a God who lived in the dirt, and died a horrible death to reconcile and gather his sheep into his fold.

Jesus loves me, loves me still,
Even though I'm weak and ill,
From his shining throne on high,
Comes to watch me where I lie.
Yes, Jesus loves me.
Yes, Jesus loves me.
Yes, Jesus loves me.
The Bible tells me so.

*Dear **Shepherd**, it is unbearable to see the damage wreaked by sin in the hearts of men. Help us to see our own sin, lay down our life, and follow you in the midst of daily challenges and temptations. Give me wisdom to know how to be an advocate and the shepherd to the sheep you have entrusted to me.*

remembering

Most of us have some really neat God moments when we know his hand has worked on a given situation. It can be easy to forget these when we are in the midst of a challenging situation or ongoing problem. This week **MELISSA SANDS** helps us focus on **remembering** some of those milestones in our own adoption journeys as we look at the Israelites, as they placed stones in the Jordan River as a reminder of what the Lord had done. These stones were to serve as a reminder when their children asked questions in the future.

SCRIPTURE FOCUS //JOSHUA 4:2-9 (NIV)

"Choose twelve men from among the people, one from each tribe, and tell them to take up twelve stones from the middle of the Jordan, from right where the priests are standing, and carry them over with you and put them down at the place where you stay tonight." So Joshua called together the twelve men he had appointed from the Israelites, one from each tribe, and said to them, "Go over before the ark of the LORD your God into the middle of the Jordan. Each of you is to take up a stone on his shoulder, according to the number of the tribes of the Israelites, to serve as a sign among you. In the future, when your children ask you, 'What do these stones mean?' tell them that the flow of the Jordan was cut off before the ark of the covenant of the LORD. When it crossed the Jordan, the waters of the Jordan were cut off. These stones are to be a memorial to the people of Israel forever."

So the Israelites did as Joshua commanded them. They took twelve stones from the middle of the Jordan, according to the number of the tribes of the Israelites, as the LORD had told Joshua; and they carried them over with them to their camp, where they put them down. Joshua set up the twelve stones that had been in the middle of the Jordan at the spot where the priests who carried the ark of the covenant had stood. And they are there to this day.

DAY 1 //remembering

The children of Israel had been on a long journey. They had been wandering in the wilderness for 40 years waiting for their time to get to the Promised Land. Moses got to sneak a peek at it (Deuteronomy 34:4) but it was Joshua who would actually lead the people across the Jordan into it. Some pretty incredible things had happened up to this point to get the Israelites where they were going; God had parted the Red Sea (Exodus 14:15-31), they had gotten free food in the form of manna (Exodus 16), and water flowed from a rock (Exodus 17).

These were not your everyday sort of events. *These were things that pointed back to the sovereignty of God.*

In early 2006, we started our adventure with adoption paperwork. Our omniscient God really did have all the details worked out, even though we couldn't always see it as such along the way. Our son had just turned one and the general adoption process was taking an average of six to eighteen months, after a dossier was in China. So we figured we'd have our daughter by the time our son was three. *Perfect family: a boy and a girl, with kids close in age.* Things generally went well through our initial paperwork stage. When there were hiccups along the way I clung to what other adoptive parents said about paperwork, "You will forget all of that once you have your daughter."

I saw God answer some pretty specific prayers like "please don't let me get lost in Washington D.C. while I get the remaining stamps on our dossier." I knew how to navigate the train and the Metro system, but was a little sketchy about getting a taxi from the State Department to the Chinese Embassy. *God provides.*

At the State Department, I struck up a conversation with a Caucasian mom and a very Asian looking daughter. It turned out she was there because she was getting her papers stamped for her second adoption and was heading to the Chinese Embassy next. She offered to drive me to the Embassy. God provided an Audi, instead of a taxi, and a cute little Chinese girl to make me **remember** that adopting from China was in his plan, and of course, he would work out the details.

I think of Mary, after Jesus was born. It says in Luke 2:19 (NIV) that she "*treasured up all these things and pondered them in her heart.*" I did a lot of pondering in those early days. I also kept a journal, so when the tough days of waiting came I would have some things to look back on, just like the Israelites **remembering** their great miracles.

Dear Lord, Thank you for the ways that you provide for us in the little details of life. Help us to remember to thank you for the ways that you show us your grace each day in the little and big things of life.

DAY 2 //remembering

We were quick with our dossier paperwork. I was proud of the fact that we finished in four months what we had been told would take six. God provided things like in-laws arriving a day earlier so that we could drive to our state's capital to get yet another stamp on paperwork, and cut a week out of our schedule. He showed us his grace in so many little ways like that. Then, our dossier was ready to go to our agency on our wedding anniversary. I saw this as another blessing from the Lord as we hit the milestone on a day that already held significance in our household. That definitely was **remembered** in my journal.

There was also this adoption seminar commercial running on our local Christian radio station at the time. I saw it as another confirmation from God that we were on the right track with this adoption. I would get flustered with the paperwork, then turn on the car at the same moment the commercial was playing, only to hear the parent speaking say, "...when we brought home our daughter Lexi..." Of all the names for them to say... the same name that we had chosen for our daughter? *I became emotional every time.* God seemed to always know which specific day I needed that commercial to play again, to give me the **reminder** that this adoption was part of his plan for our family. This was another memory to jot down in my journal.

After we completed the initial paperwork, the true waiting began. Oh, was that hard. With a pregnancy you know you will have your child in nine months. With adoption, you will get your child in _____ months or even years? Remember all of that paperwork? Remember how you acknowledged that there are no certainties in adoptions? Yes, I loathed the paperwork at this point, *because it reminded me that we really didn't know what we were getting into.* A few months into our wait, the amount of referrals coming in each month significantly dropped off. What used to be a joyous email update from our agency telling us how many families got referrals—as each referral moved us closer to our own—turned to sadness at the lack of progress.

What happened to our plan of having that perfect little family with a boy and girl close in age? As our son's third birthday approached, we found we needed to resubmit a new home study because of the extended wait. At times it didn't seem like God had a real handle on what was going on with this adoption thing. But then a verse that I have always treasured would bubble to the surface. Jeremiah 29:11 (NIV) says *"For I know the plans I have for you," declares the LORD, "plans to prosper you and not to harm you, plans to give you hope and a future."* I had to constantly **remember** this truth, even if I didn't particularly feel like it in the moment: I believe in God's sovereignty and his glorious plans for me.

Dear Lord, Thank you that you have a plan for my life and a plan for my adopted child. Please help us to remember this even on the days when we don't necessarily feel it. Thank you for knowing my future.

DAY 3 //remembering

Christmas of 2008 was bittersweet. On one hand, it was a happy time to **remember** our glorious Savior's birth. Luke 2:11-12 says, *"Today in the town of David a Savior has been born to you; he is the Messiah, the Lord. This will be a sign to you: You will find a baby wrapped in cloths and lying in a manger."* This is Good News worth rejoicing!

On the other hand, it was difficult to hear songs like "All I Really Want" by Steven Curtis Chapman on the radio.

All I really want for Christmas
Is someone to tuck me in
A shoulder to cry on if I lose
Shoulders to ride on if I win
There's so much I could ask for
But there's just one thing I need
All I really want for Christmas is a family

I was beyond ready to tuck our little girl in at night. I wanted to be singing that song with happy tears because our baby girl had come home, instead of wallowing in the sadness of not having her yet.

And then I found out we had gotten pregnant. Seriously? This wasn't in "our plan." One of the benefits of adopting, I had surmised, was we would get to skip over the newborn stage of sleepless nights.

We went through the emotional roller coaster of excitement over a new baby, to losing that baby, to quickly getting pregnant again in the span of a few months. Right before Christmas, the following year, we were blessed with our dear daughter, Lexi. She was perfect in every way, and yet she had blond hair and a lot lighter skin than the Asian version of our daughter that we had imagined for so many years.

In Isaiah 55:8 (NLT), God describes why I can't always see or imagine what he is doing. *"My thoughts are nothing like your thoughts," says the LORD. "And my ways are far beyond anything you could imagine."* This was my **reminder** that God had this thing under control.

And just like the Israelites probably didn't like all that wandering in the wilderness, he was preparing them in his time for something good... *The Promised Land.* I still felt like we were wandering in the wilderness of adoption, but for now it was God's plan for us to wander a little longer... with two kids in tow.

Dear Lord, on those days when our plans don't seem to match up perfectly with what you are doing, please send me a reminder that your ways are not my ways and that you are making a way in the wilderness for me. Please give me the grace to follow your ways and not my own because you know the plans you have for me.

DAY 4 //remembering

Sometimes you can be in the wilderness for a really long time. It stinks. I don't wish it upon anyone. I'm guessing the Israelites probably said, on more than one occasion, to Moses—are we there yet? *But there are lessons to be learned in the waiting.*

Perhaps God chooses to give us moments of refreshment, to provide endurance *to go the distance* during those tough seasons. One of those times came to us in the form of a job opportunity. My husband's employment moved us to Canada for a year. We saw this as a missional opportunity from God, as well as a little respite from doing home study updates.

We packed up our winter gear and headed north. God gave us some great family **memories** that year. I can now see how much we would have missed if the adoption process for China wasn't so slow at the time.

Towards the end of that year, I started to get restless again as I envisioned returning home to the emotional and financial burdens that come along with an in-progress adoption. I was not looking forward to picking up the paperwork trail.

One day I asked God for a sign. Psalm 86:17 (NIV) says *"Give me a sign of your goodness, that my enemies may see it and be put to shame, for you, LORD, have helped me and comforted me."* I needed to be comforted that day. I needed to be **reminded** once again that this adoption was right for us. I was very specific as I prayed, "Please God—just show me something in *black and white* so I will know we should continue with this process." I had all of these **memories** of things he had done in the past, but I needed another stone to add to the pile.

The very next day, I sat reading my Beth Moore Bible study on the book of Esther. Right there in *black and white* were the words to Steven Curtis Chapman's song "Miracle of the Moment." Wow! Lately I'd been encouraged listening to this song whenever I was discouraged with our adoption process, and then I read the very same lyrics in my study guide:

There's a wonder in the here and now
It's right there in front of you
I don't want you to miss the miracle of the moment

I knew it was God singing this to my heart, **reminding** me of all the other good things that were going on in my life at the time. It was a comforting reminder to live each day with the miracle of that moment and that God would give me future miracles in our adoption process down the road. I could still enjoy today's treasures while waiting for tomorrow's blessings.

Dear Lord, Thank you for signs of your goodness. Please help me to remember these. Thank you for comforting me in your own special way when I need reminders that you are the ultimate comforter and provider of my needs.

DAY 5 //remembering

I love that God can usually take our simple prayers and turn it into something more than we could have asked for or imagined. Just a few days after I had my answer in "black and white," God **reminded** me he can do even better than that. I headed to church to watch the next video session for the Esther Bible study, only to see Beth Moore wearing what appeared to me to be a very Chinese-looking shirt. Now this might seem insignificant to you, but I believe God only intended it to hold significance *for me* on that day.

I heard God telling me... you ask for something in black and white and I did that. But the truth of the matter is that I can do way better than that. I can give you your sign in bold, vivid colors (her shirt definitely was!).

I wrote in my journal "God's like that—out-giving what we even imagine as good." One of the verses that I've had memorized since high school is Ephesians 3:20 *"Now to him who is able to do immeasurably more than all we ask or imagine, according to his power that is at work within us, to him be glory in the church and in Christ Jesus throughout all generations, for ever and ever! Amen."*

God can use something, as simple as a colorful Asian-inspired shirt, to remind us of his higher ways. This was just another rock to put on my pile of stories that I want to tell my daughter as she grows older. Like in Joshua 4:6 (NIV) *"In the future, when your children ask you, 'What do these stones mean?'"* I want her to see the times where God kept **reminding** me that one day he would bring her to our family.

It took over five-and-a-half years, but one day we did receive that phone call telling us about our new daughter. Oh my goodness, that cute little face in the pictures they sent! Forget adding a stone to that day... bring in the mega boulder!

So take a few minutes and think about those stones that God has put in your path that you want to share with your children. Write them down, ponder them in your heart. Be like Joshua and the Israelites and go outside and get a rock to set on your counter to remind you of the treasure that you have in your adopted child. They can serve as good **reminders** on the tough days of parenting... and life.

Dear Lord, May we always remember the ways that you give us things that are above and beyond what we could ask or imagine. May we tell these stories to our children and others for the glory of your name. Amen. Hallelujah!

peace

When **ALLISON CUNNINGHAM**'s husband first suggested they adopt a nine-year-old orphan in Nicaragua, she had anything but **peace**. And yet, God eventually brought her to a place of total peace about the adoption, adding to her family, and an 800-mile move in the middle of it all. This week, she shares how focusing on God's sovereign Lordship, and Jesus' powerful name, can help us all find **peace**, no matter our circumstances.

SCRIPTURE FOCUS //PHILIPPIANS 4:4-9 (NIV)

Rejoice in the Lord always. I will say it again: Rejoice! Let your gentleness be evident to all. The Lord is near. Do not be anxious about anything, but in everything, by prayer and petition, with thanksgiving, present your requests to God. And the peace of God, which transcends all understanding, will guard your hearts and your minds in Christ Jesus. Finally, brothers, whatever is true, whatever is noble, whatever is right, whatever is pure, whatever is lovely, whatever is admirable—if anything is excellent or praiseworthy—think about such things. Whatever you have learned or received or heard from me, or seen in me--put it into practice. And the God of peace will be with you.

DAY 1 //*peace*

What do you do when your husband comes home from a mission trip and states that he has met our daughter, when we had never talked about adoption? I had to grab ahold of the Lordship of Jesus. *Rejoice in the Lord always. I will say it again: Rejoice!* Because of the death and resurrection of Jesus, we have 24/7 access to God. This truth is worthy of our most exuberant praise. God's heart toward us is loving kindness and his ways are always good.

No matter what our circumstances are, the unchanging, always faithful Lordship of Jesus remains.

For me this reality was what I had to cling to when that one conversation flipped my world upside down. We have two biological sons and adoption was never a discussion or plan for us. I was completely blindsided with his declaration. My mental clarity was thrown out the window. My heart was sent into a tailspin.

Before this late January conversation, I had just completed a twenty-one day fast. During that fast I was praying for direction for the year and seeking God's heart. Never once did God say anything about adoption. *Not. one.word.* As I think back to those days, I'm not sure if I was more upset that God was disrupting my plans or that he didn't give me a heads up! Realizing my position as a child of the King, I had to realign my heart under the Lordship of Christ. As my Savior, he is worthy of every part of my life and as Lord, he can change my plans to keep in step with his plan.

It is a conscious decision to yield to Christ when plans change and life feels out of control. Especially in the adoption journey, this is a choice made over and over and over again. After many tears of grieving my own desires, processing the difficulties I could foresee and coming to a place of being willing to pay the price, I submitted myself to God's plan and we began the process of adopting our daughter.

It felt like backward free falling into a swimming pool. And just like the water catches your body and encapsulates your being upon contact, the Lord is so gracious and tender to sustain and hold our lives.

In the myriad of emotions felt, to the seemingly endless wait and even in exhilaration of fruition, do I allow my soul to be ruled by *the instability of the process* or to be held secure by *an unchanging God* who is with me always? **Peace** comes when we relinquish control of what we cannot make happen on our own, trusting God's ultimate authority in our lives. He is the Almighty. He is faithful. His peace will be our guide as we follow him.

Father, forgive my selfishness. I give you control over my life, and accept the **peace** *that comes from putting you completely in charge. Thank you for sustaining me and holding me close. Amen.*

DAY 2 //peace

Through delayed answers, piles of paperwork, lists of preparations, scattered emotions, increased financial responsibility, and months of waiting, we have many opportunities to give into chaos and become overwhelmed. However, this is not our only option! Philippians 4:5-6 reminds us the Lord is near. It states: *Let your gentleness be evident to all. The Lord is near. 6 Do not be anxious about anything, but in everything, by prayer and petition, with thanksgiving, present your requests to God.*

This is not a vague, overarching truth but one that calls us to awareness of God's presence in the details of our lives. Furthermore, our loving God invites us to bring everything that weighs heavy on our hearts and minds to him. The question is not whether God can handle the anxious thoughts, insurmountable tasks, or weighty decisions we carry, but do we trust him to be true to his word?

Do not fear, for I am with you; Do not anxiously look about you, for I am your God. I will strengthen you, surely I will help you, Surely I will uphold you with My righteous right hand. —Isaiah 41:10 (NASB)

I am the Lord, the God of all mankind. Is anything too hard for me? —Jeremiah 32:27 (NIV)

In the day when I cried out, you answered me, And made me bold with strength in my soul. —Psalm 138:3 (NKJV)

The Lord will perfect that which concerns me; your mercy, O LORD, endures forever; Do not forsake the works of your hands. —Psalm 138:8 (NKJV)

The Lord will guide you continually, And satisfy your soul in drought, And strengthen your bones; you shall be like a watered garden, And like a spring of water, whose waters do not fail. —Isaiah 58:11 (NKJV)

Peace and trust go hand in hand. One of the major areas in which we had to trust God during our adoption process was with our finances. Frankly, we didn't have the thousands of dollars we knew it would take. Trusting that God would provide, we decided at the beginning of the journey to take one step at a time. Each time we needed to submit documents with their fees, we had the money.

Then came the translation of our dossier and the money was not there! Putting our trust in God's word, we thanked Jesus that he had provided up to that point and prayed he would continue. Would we continue to trust him or get frantic? We prayed and waited. Then one day we got a phone call from someone wanting to be part of our adoption journey through a financial gift that paid for the translation! He provided!

Jesus, I pray for an exchange of worry for peace. You are faithful even when I am not. May the truth of who you are quiet my heart and make me steadfast in your all sufficiency. Amen.

DAY 3 //peace

We place value on a name. Before we have a baby, we research what names mean, origins, think about family heritage and if someone we don't like has a particular name, it is out! Even when adopting a child, we think about their birth name. Its significance is of interest, as well as what impact it may have on his or her future. Decisions are made whether to change it or let it remain.

Our daughter's name is Rosmeri. Upon receiving her paperwork, we learned her official name was Rosemary. She had never actually seen her name written so she wrote her name phonetically, "Rosmeri." Because she was nine and the changes adoption brings are many, we decided to make the spelling she is comfortable with her official name. We may not be successful in finding personalized souvenirs in gift shops, but keeping her name was significant in steadying her heart. While that decision was of singular impact, there is another name that once written on a heart, changes everything. It is significant enough to not only change our destiny but also our perspective and how we navigate life.

Jesus.

Before he ever made his entrance to the Earth, his name was prophesied. In Isaiah 9:6: *And his name will be called Wonderful, Counselor, Mighty God, Everlasting Father, Prince of **Peace***. In Galatians, one of the fruits of God's Spirit is **peace**. It's who he is. Philippians 4:7 reminds us that *the **peace** of God, which transcends all understanding, will guard your hearts and minds in Christ Jesus*. Without Jesus Christ there is no **peace**. It surpasses our understanding because **peace** is a supernatural gift of God. In the same way we receive salvation from Jesus through faith, we must also accept the gift of **peace** through faith.

There are many ways we look for **peace**. We search for it in money, position, status, possessions, relationships, substances, charity work, control and the list could go on and on. In our striving, we only end up weary and worn. The truth is that Jesus is the only source of **peace**. In John 14:27 Jesus says, "***Peace** I leave with you; my **peace** I give to you. I do not give to you as the world gives. Do not let your hearts be troubled and do not be afraid.*"

Friend, look no further. Let your wandering mind halt and recognize that Jesus is here waiting for you. Jesus, *the Prince of **Peace***, offers you the gift himself. He willingly invites you to lay the burdens you carry upon him. Jesus is where **peace** begins and where it never ends. He is limitless and his supply never runs dry.

Jesus, thank you for carrying my burdens, and for providing the peace that passes all understanding. Guard my heart and mind with thoughts only of you. Amen.

DAY 4 //peace

It was April when we sent our first correspondence to Nicaragua to begin the process of making a nine-year-old little girl our daughter. Just two months later, my husband received an offer to work for the corporate office of his company. We prayed and knew it was an open door we needed to walk through. We had challenges including major house projects under way, our home study had already been completed using our current home, and our responsibilities in our church were many. None of this would have mattered, except the corporate office was 800 miles away in a different state!

In the four weeks before his start date, with much help from friends, we completed the unfinished projects, renovated a bathroom, stepped down from leadership in our church and tried to prepare our children for what would be the most difficult season of our lives. The questions and uncertainty threatened to devastate me. Yet I was anchored by the one thing that is true beyond a shadow of a doubt.

I belong to Jesus.

The truth of his word was the only sure thing I could hold onto and at times it was a fight to keep my mind steadfast.

Hebrews 4:12 (NIV) says, *"For the word of God is alive and active. Sharper than any double-edged sword, it penetrates even to dividing soul and spirit, joints and marrow; it judges the thoughts and attitudes of the heart."*

This is important because when life overwhelms, we need the Holy Spirit to expose the lies and fears that would captivate us and steal our **peace**. Philippians 4:8 encourages us to think about *whatever is true, whatever is noble, whatever is right, whatever is pure, whatever is lovely, whatever is admirable, anything is excellent or praiseworthy*. When we keep our thoughts on these things, then the **peace** of God will be with us.

It's cause and effect. The cause is our thoughts; the effect is **peace**.

It's an action with a promise. The battle for **peace** is waged in the mind. The weapon is our thoughts.

Do we allow unproductiveness by rehearsing the what-ifs that may never come to pass or take hold of the promise of God by training our internal dialogue to focus on what is true, pure and excellent? **Peace** is for today. The adoption journey is filled with waiting for what will come, dreams of the future and anticipating the tomorrows. We can't allow what awaits to steal the **peace** available to you now.

Father God, thank you for providing perfect peace when my mind is stayed on you. I trust you, my Lord, my Rock eternal. Amen.

DAY 5 //peace

There is a familiar saying, "practice makes perfect." In recent years it's been modified to "practice makes progress." Based on our theme scripture from Philippians 4:4-9, I suggest that "practice brings **peace**!"

Paul exhorts us in this text to practice bringing our requests to God as well as to think on things that are true, noble, praise worthy and of a good report. It is not enough to merely have knowledge or understanding of God's word. James 1:22 (NIV) says, "*Do not merely listen to the word and so deceive yourselves. Do what it says.*" The key that unlocks access to **peace** is the practice of disregarding thoughts that do not line up with God's word in exchange for truth.

One day after our adoption was complete and the integration of our daughter into our family was in full swing, I was in total meltdown status. All three of my children needed my attention to complete their homework and dinner needed to be made. My husband, now working in another state, was calling on the phone for his daily talk time, and I was caught in the middle of it all! *Where is the pause on life button when you need it?*

I was screaming for God to rescue me. When the height of frustration and the feeling that I was not enough threatened to consume me, I heard the Holy Spirit say, "*Be a contender.*" Immediately, this scripture came to mind and I knew what God was communicating: *For though we live in the world, we do not wage war as the world does. The weapons we fight with are not the weapons of the world. On the contrary, they have divine power to demolish strongholds. We demolish arguments and every pretension that sets itself up against the knowledge of God, and we take captive every thought to make it obedient to Christ.* —2 Corinthians 10:3-5 (NIV)

The battle for peace is won and lost in our mind. We say: "Nothing ever works out..." He says: No! *And we know that in all things God works for the good of those who love him, who have been called according to his purpose.* —Romans 8:28 (NIV)

"I can't do this anymore..." *My grace is sufficient for you, for my power is made perfect in weakness...* —2 Corinthians 12:9a (NIV)

"I am so afraid..." *God has not given us a spirit of fear but a spirit of power, of love and a sound mind.* —2 Timothy 1:7 (NKJV)

Submitting thoughts to Christ takes practice. However, it is worth it! As you train your mind to think on what is true, you will experience **peace** like never before. Jesus loves you, his plan for you is good and his mercies never fail. Hold onto his word and likewise, be a contender for **peace**!

*Prince of **Peace**, thank you for providing grace and **peace** no matter what my circumstances. May this truth always calm my spirit and bring me closer to you. Amen.*

love

Ultimately, **love** is the reason we adopt, right? Without **love**, God's **love**, it would be impossible for parents to bring children into their home that do not have their same features, share their medical history, or grow in their belly. **Love** is the reason we call these children *ours*. When we understand the **love** God has for us, His children, we are then able to freely **love** our children and their birth families out of that overflow. This week, **JESSICA SATTERFIELD** will share different stories throughout Scripture where God clearly showed His love to His people.

SCRIPTURE FOCUS //DAY 1

Now Sarai, Abram's wife, had borne him no children. She had a female Egyptian servant whose name was Hagar. And Sarai said to Abram, "Behold now, the Lord has prevented me from bearing children. Go in to my servant; it may be that I shall obtain children by her." And Abram listened to the voice of Sarai. So, after Abram had lived ten years in the land of Canaan, Sarai, Abram's wife, took Hagar the Egyptian, her servant, and gave her to Abram her husband as a wife. And he went in to Hagar, and she conceived. And when she saw that she had conceived, she looked with contempt on her mistress. And Sarai said to Abram, "May the wrong done to me be on you! I gave my servant to your embrace, and when she saw that she had conceived, she looked on me with contempt. May the Lord judge between you and me!" But Abram said to Sarai, "Behold, your servant is in your power; do to her as you please." Then Sarai dealt harshly with her, and she fled from her.

The angel of the Lord found her by a spring of water in the wilderness, the spring on the way to Shur. And he said, "Hagar, servant of Sarai, where have you come from and where are you going?" She said, "I am fleeing from my mistress Sarai." The angel of the Lord said to her, "Return to your mistress and submit to her." The angel of the Lord also said to her, "I will surely multiply your offspring so that they cannot be numbered for multitude." And the angel of the Lord said to her, "Behold, you are pregnant and shall bear a son. You shall call his name Ishmael, because the Lord has listened to your affliction. He shall be a wild donkey of a man, his hand against everyone and everyone's hand against him, and he shall dwell over against all his kinsmen."

So she called the name of the Lord who spoke to her, "You are a God of seeing," for she said, "Truly here I have seen him who looks after me." Therefore the well was called Beer-lahai-roi; it lies between Kadesh and Bered.

And Hagar bore Abram a son, and Abram called the name of his son, whom Hagar bore, Ishmael. Abram was eighty-six years old when Hagar bore Ishmael to Abram.(Genesis 16:1-16 NASB)

SCRIPTURE FOCUS //DAY 2

"Therefore, behold, I will allure her, and bring her into the wilderness, and speak tenderly to her. And there I will give her her vineyards and make the Valley of Achor a door of hope. And there she shall answer as in the days of her youth, as at the time when she came out of the land of Egypt.

"And in that day, declares the Lord, you will call me 'My Husband,' and no longer will you call me 'My Baal.' For I will remove the names of the Baals from her mouth, and they shall be remembered by name no more. And I will make for them a covenant on that day with the beasts of the field, the birds of the heavens, and the creeping things of the ground. And I will abolish the bow, the sword, and war from the land, and I will make you lie down in safety. And I will betroth you to me forever. I will betroth you to me in righteousness and in justice, in steadfast love and in mercy. I will betroth you to me in faithfulness. And you shall know the Lord.

"And in that day I will answer, declares the Lord, I will answer the heavens, and they shall answer the earth, and the earth shall answer the grain, the wine, and the oil, and they shall answer Jezreel, and I will sow her for myself in the land. And I will have mercy on No Mercy, and I will say to Not My People, 'You are my people'; and he shall say, 'You are my God.'" (Hosea 2:14-23)

SCRIPTURE FOCUS //DAY 3

Now Thomas, one of the Twelve, called the Twin, was not with them when Jesus came. So the other disciples told him, "We have seen the Lord." But he said to them, "Unless I see in his hands the mark of the nails, and place my finger into the mark of the nails, and place my hand into his side, I will never believe."

Eight days later, his disciples were inside again, and Thomas was with them. Although the doors were locked, Jesus came and stood among them and said, "Peace be with you." Then he said to Thomas, "Put your finger here, and see my hands; and put out your hand, and place it in my side. Do not disbelieve, but believe." Thomas answered him, "My Lord and my God!" Jesus said to him, "Have you believed because you have seen me? Blessed are those who have not seen and yet have believed." (John 20:24-29 NASB)

SCRIPTURE FOCUS //DAY 4

But Jesus went to the Mount of Olives. Early in the morning he came again to the temple. All the people came to him, and he sat down and taught them. The scribes and the Pharisees brought a woman who had been caught in adultery, and placing her in the midst they said to him, "Teacher, this woman has been caught in the act of adultery. Now in the Law Moses commanded us to stone such women. So what do you say?"

This they said to test him, that they might have some charge to bring against him. Jesus bent down and wrote with his finger on the ground. And as they continued to ask him, he stood up and said to them, "Let him who is without sin among you be the first to throw a stone at her." And once more he bent down and wrote on the ground. But when they heard it, they went away one by one, beginning with the older ones, and Jesus was left alone with the woman standing before him.

Jesus stood up and said to her, "Woman, where are they? Has no one condemned you?" She said, "No one, Lord." And Jesus said, "Neither do I condemn you; go, and from now on sin no more." (John 8:1-11 NASB)

SCRIPTURE FOCUS //DAY 5

Surely he has borne our griefs
*   and carried our sorrows;*
yet we esteemed him stricken,
*   smitten by God, and afflicted.*
But he was pierced for our transgressions;
*   he was crushed for our iniquities;*
upon him was the chastisement that brought us peace,
*   and with his wounds we are healed.*
All we like sheep have gone astray;
*   we have turned—every one—to his own way;*
and the Lord has laid on him
*   the iniquity of us all. (Isaiah 53:4-6)*

DAY 1 //love

For years, I have always identified with Sarah, Abraham's wife. Barren myself, I look at her life and can understand her. However, in Genesis 16, I find myself in Hagar's shoes. Hagar was Sarah's maidservant. Unlike Sarah, Hagar's womb was open, and because of this, Sarah "dealt with her harshly." Hagar was a young girl with nothing. No title. No family. No future. Now she found herself out of a job, homeless, and pregnant with her boss' son. I can't imagine her despair.

Sometimes I feel as if I'm doing this all wrong. Being a mama is hard. My dishes are piled in my sink as I type this. I had to dig through dirty clothes that were in the floor to find pajamas for my baby because the flu has overtaken our house this week. It's Monday and I haven't bought groceries for the week. Toys are scattered all over my living room and if I hear Mickey Mouse Clubhouse one more time, I think I might scream.

However, these are insignificant to the despairs you might be feeling today. **Loving** children that come from hard places is difficult. You might have numerous therapy appointments scheduled this week. You might feel as if you're the only parent who is still having trouble bonding with your child. You might feel as if this calling to adopt has taken you out in a wilderness and left you with nothing but pain, like Hagar.

But God didn't leave her there.

The angel of the Lord found her. He called her by name, "*Hagar, servant of Sarai, where have you come from and where are you going?*" He saw her. The God of the universe saw her there in that wilderness, and called her by name! She named that place, Beer-lahai-roi, "You are a God of seeing."

Sweet friend, whatever desert you find yourself in today, know he sees you. Because of his **love** for you, he will not leave you there. He knows where you have been, and knows where you are going, just like Hagar.

Sometimes we just need to be seen. Precious one, he sees your dirty dishes, your tight schedule, and your hard child. And he **loves** you there. Right where you are.

*Lord, I'm praising you today for being the God who sees. You see the real me. You see my mess and all my hard. You also see the bright future you have planned for me and the beautiful hope I have in you. Thank you for **loving** me here, right where I am. Let me rest in your love today.*

DAY 2 //love

"God doesn't want something from us. He simply wants us." —C.S. Lewis

The center doors open to reveal a beautiful bride dressed in white, with a face radiating joy and expectancy of new life with her beloved. As everyone's gaze is set upon her entrance, mine centers on the groom. Standing in his most handsome suit, he wipes away the tears of **love** that drip down his cheek. There it begins, husband and wife. A relationship so intimate, that, words cannot describe.

Hosea writes the most beautiful **love** story, perfectly paralleling the gospel. It is the story of a bride who cannot keep her covenant. Choosing, over and over again, other things that merely pale in comparison to the beauty of what is already hers. A loving and faithful husband who chooses, over and over again, to relentlessly pursue his bride, no matter her response.

Thinking of the whole story of Hosea, slowly read today's Scripture, allowing the words to press deep into your heart.

Therefore, behold, I will allure her, and lead her into the wilderness, and speak tenderly to her... And in that day, declares the Lord, you will call me "My Husband," and no longer will you call me "My Baal"... I will betroth you to me in faithfulness. And you shall know the Lord... and I will say to Not My People, "You are my People," and he shall say, "You are my God."

That's me. The prostitute who continuously chooses other things that only pale in comparison to him. And that's him. The faithful husband who has a **love** for me that is jealous and wild. And even when he knows I will still choose other things, His **love** is relentless. Not giving up. He still wants me.

God wants you today, precious one. You may find yourself in a wilderness that looks all too lonely. It is there, in the hard places, he whispers of his great **love** for you. He takes your hand and even leads you there to be with him. He says to you today, "Don't call me any other name, but husband. Because that is how close I want to be to you."

He is a beautiful husband. Let your hair down with him, nestle up close to his chest today, and listen to the cadence of his **love** for you. It is relentless.

*My Beloved, thank you for always choosing me, even when I don't choose you. I praise you today for your relentless **love** for me. Give me strength to open the deepest parts of my heart to you. I barely know you; take me deeper. Let me hear your whispers of **love** over me today.*

DAY 3 //love

Now Thomas, one of the Twelve, called the Twin, was not with them when Jesus came. So the other disciples told him, "We have seen the Lord," But he said to them, "Unless I see in his hands the mark of the nail, and place my finger into the mark of the nails, and place my hand into his side, I will never believe." Eight days later, his disciples were inside again, and Thomas was with them. Although the doors were locked, Jesus came and stood among them and said, "Peace be with you," Then he said to Thomas," Put your finger here, and see my hands; and put out your hand, and place it in my side. Do not disbelieve, but believe," Thomas answered him, "My Lord and my God!" Jesus said to him, "Have you believed because you have seen me? Blessed are those who have not seen and yet have believed." —John 20:24-29

There have been more times I have doubted, during our adoptions, than times I have believed.

When we were waiting every single month for that positive test, and it once again proved to label me "barren," I doubted God's goodness to me. When we were waiting for what seemed like forever to be matched with our birth mom, I doubted God would answer our prayer. When each payment was due to our agency or lawyers, I doubted God's provision. When our birth mom chose us and we waited six weeks wondering if she would really go through with it, I doubted that God could really be that good. After our daughter was home, and I was learning how to be a mom, I doubted God picked the right girl. When we experienced our first failed adoption, I doubted God's calling.

Whether I like it or not, Thomas and I share a good bit in common. Thomas altogether doubted Christ's resurrection. I'm sure he had his reasons, but it just didn't make sense to him. He had to see Jesus for himself, feel his side, and see his scars. Jesus, in his **love** and kindness towards Thomas, showed him his wounds. He placed his hand on His side, just what Thomas needed. For years I thought Jesus showed up to that room as a chance to prove Thomas wrong. But he showed up for Thomas out of his **love**.

What are you doubting today? Are you doubting God will show up for you, answer your prayers, provide, and be good to you? Whatever it is, Jesus **loves** you in it. And he will show up today right in your doubt. He says to you, "Peace be with you. Do not disbelieve; *believe*."

*Risen Lord, so often I find myself doubting you. Thank you for **loving** me in my doubt. Speak peace over my heart and allow me the grace to trust that You are Who You say you are. Thank you for meeting me in my doubt. Help me to believe and heal my disbelief.*

DAY 4 //love

"There is no pit so deep that God's love is not deeper still." —Corrie Ten Boom

Her heart was beating out of her chest as she looked in the face of the one who would choose if she lived or died. Fearing for her life, she stood there, barely dressed in the church full of men. She felt every stare and heard every snicker as a sea of people cleared the way for her "unclean" self to move through. She stood there exposed, feeling vulnerable, ashamed, and judged.

He bent down, the one with the kind face, and started writing things in the sand. Suddenly, the men, one by one, lowered their heads and began walking away, until it was just them. *"Woman, where are they? Has no one condemned you? Neither do I condemn you; go, and from now on sin no more."*

Those words, "Neither do I condemn you," meet my heart in a desperate place. So often I feel like this woman: Not enough, ashamed, and judged. On days I lose patience so easily with my little girl. The times I snap at my husband. When I feel like I cannot give my dad one more ounce of grace. The bitterness I sometimes feel from my barren womb. All of these and many more are one thing... sin. And he meets me here, in my sin. He says to me, "Neither do I condemn you."

This kind-faced man rescues me over and over again in my sin. Sweet sister, he rescues you too. Whether it's the same sin you feel there will never be victory over, or your sin looks similar to some of mine, we do not live in condemnation! Because of the Father's immeasurable and unending love for us, we are free through Jesus' sacrifice on the cross. Read John 8:1-11 and let his words, reign true over your heart today.

*Sweet Jesus, thank you that your **love** is so great for me and that, through the cross, you have given me freedom from my sin. Because of your **love** for me, I do not have to live ashamed, guilty, or judged. In you alone, I have freedom from sin's death grip. Please convict me of the sin in my heart that separates me from you. Give me the courage to turn from that sin, and give me victory over it. Holy Spirit, whisper your words in this story over my heart today, reminding me of who I was before you, and who I am now because of your great **love**. Your face is so kind, and your **love** for my wayward heart, is deeper still. I **love** you.*

DAY 5 //love

"You've picked the wrong girl, Lord," I said in the shower, as tears and hot water ran over my face. After a long day of hard, sometimes it really feels that way. At times, I barely feel like I am surviving. I struggle to be a good wife. I'm an exhausted working mama to a baby I prayed for and so desperately wanted. Very soon, I will have another child that will call me mommy, but never felt kick inside me. God has called me to a community of women to whom I often feel inadequate to lead. I fall into bed exhausted at night, feeling poured out more times than filled. And I hear those words, and often believe them. "You've picked the wrong girl."

This week we have seen story, after beautiful story, of God's **love** displayed through his people. God's **love** meets us right where we are in the most intimate ways. His **love** reaches past our doubt and rescues us from our sin. Oh how we would be dismayed if we didn't look at Jesus, and the Father's ultimate declaration of his **love** for us.

The whole Bible tells the story of this **Love**. Isaiah so beautifully tells us that Jesus took upon himself our grief. He carried our sorrows. He was pierced for our sins, Yahweh's Beloved Son. It is only by his wounds we are free. His stripes bring to us healing. This is **love**, friend. That the Father would put to death his Son, to adopt you and me into his family. So we might know him. And know of his **love** for us.

When I was crying out to him in the shower, reminding him of all the reasons he picked the wrong girl for this job, I kept telling him I bring him nothing. There is nothing left in me to give. And isn't that true? My greatest days of Kingdom work are only filthy rags. My very best wife skills and parenting strategies are merely pathetic attempts. And he is okay with that, because he purchased me knowing I had nothing to offer him. I don't owe him anything; Jesus paid it all for me. His beautiful sacrifice looks the Father in the eyes, and says, "You picked the right girl, because she's mine."

Today, sweet sister, *you are enough*. Not because of what you have to offer your husband, your once-orphaned children, or even the Lord, but because of Jesus and his **love**. It is here, in his overflow, which we operate. Not by mustering up anything on our own, but out of his **love** story put on display. His **love** for you is more than you can ever imagine. His **love** is higher than the highest mountain, deeper than the deepest ocean, and wider than the equator. His **love** is vast, intimate, and relentless for you. There is no question he picked the right girl.

*Loving Father, words can never adequately describe your **love**. When I feel as if you picked the wrong girl, remind me what Jesus did. Not the story I've heard over and over, but help me see the face of the God-Man who is living and alive with scars proving your **love**. Let your **love** wreck me today, consume my thoughts, and set my heart ablaze. May I **love** the beautiful souls you have put in my life out of this overflow. You are beautiful. Take me deeper still.*

contributors

CAROLINE BAILEY //barrenness, page 27

Caroline is a mother of three children through adoption, and a strong advocate for the needs of children and families involved in the child welfare system in the United States. At the age of eleven, she underwent an emergency hysterectomy in order to save her life. Caroline is the youngest female known to have a hysterectomy.

In 2006, Caroline and her husband, Bruce, became foster parents. Through their journey of foster care, they learned so much about the needs of children, and were greatly humbled by the experience. They adopted two of their children through foster care. Their youngest child is a relative of Caroline, who they adopted in 2013.

Currently, Caroline works for a Christian child welfare agency in Missouri. She has been a guest speaker at churches and conferences regarding adoption, and is currently working on a memoir about her illness, barrenness, and the impact of faith, foster care, and adoption in her life.

Caroline shares her experience about foster care, adoption, barrenness, and faith on her blog: **BARRENTOBLESSED.WORDPRESS.COM.**

AMY BULTEMEIER //endurance, page 124

Amy is passionate about following God's purpose for her life, even though, she admits, she has not always lived that way. "There was a day when I lived in fear of all the things that *could* happen if I gave up complete control of my life. I trusted *conditionally* in God, not fully surrendered to His purpose for my life. All that changed in September of 2002, when our first son, Dawson, passed away due to conditions of his premature birth. It was during that grieving process that I turned to my faith and saw that God used that tragedy to open up a deeper relationship with Him. I try to live each day in His grace and full of gratitude."

Amy, who lives with her family in Indiana, says her children are constant reminders of God's grace, making her want to serve and bring glory to the Kingdom of God. The Bultemeiers have five children, each one brought in different circumstances. "We endured the heartache of losing a child, a difficult pregnancy that taught our family about hope in the Lord, and learning to live obediently by answering God's call to adopt from Guatemala. As we gained a better understanding of God's will in our lives we found ourselves praying for clarity on yet another international adoption." In 2014, Amy and her husband finalized the adoption of two children from Nicaragua.

AMIE COOPER //worry, page 34

As a college student, Amie spent a summer doing orphan ministry in Zambia, Africa. After graduating with her bachelor's in Family and Child Development from Liberty University, Amie pursued a full-time career in social work. But then, she became overwhelmed by the lack of foster and adoptive families within her community.

Feeling led by the Holy Spirit, Amie and her husband, Zach, became foster parents as newlyweds. They quickly opened their home to a toddler and a teen, followed by two more children, before becoming pregnant. That's right, they went from 0 to 5 children in just 2½ years! After filling up her own home, Amie began recruiting other families to foster and adopt, which led their family to South Carolina. "My heart's desire is to encourage families to pursue foster care and adoption despite the obstacles that Satan puts in their path, not the least of which is worry and anxiety," says Amie.

"I realized that at the heart of my worry was my expectation that I would have all the answers as a mother. That somehow, my mothering would fix my children's pain. The truth is that I can't fix anyone, only Jesus can do that. God is the only one who can redeem the years of abuse and neglect that my children endured before adoption."

Read more from Amie at **ADOPTIVEMOMAMIE.BLOGSPOT.COM.**

MELISSA CORKUM //self-care, page 15

"Unlike many families," admits Melissa, "my husband was the impetus for starting our adoption journey. He has had a heart for adoption since middle school and God providentially matched him with a wife who was herself adopted. I have now come full circle. As with many of yours, our adoption journey seems to have a mind of its own. Six years after a chance encounter with a waiting child list, we now have four kiddos that have joined our family through adoption."

Melissa and her husband brought a toddler home from Korea, then, against all odds, adopted three unrelated children from Ethiopia. At the time, they were 11, 13, and 14 years old. While their lives are busy homeschooling six kids (we also have two bio kids), they are also active in orphan care through their non-profit, the Grafted, and a social enterprise coffee shop, Cafe Tesfa.

Read more from Melissa at **WWW.THECORKUMS.COM.**

JESSIE CRABTREE //trust, page 54

After a few years of serving as missionaries in Nicaragua, and only about six months of trying to get pregnant, God pretty much put Yader, their Nicaraguan son, in into Jessie and her husband's laps and said, "Are you ready for this?"

"It was amazing to watch God orchestrate bringing us together as a family through some pretty awesome circumstances," shares Jessie. "We first met Yader when he was just one-month-old. At the time, he and his mother were still living in the transitional home that she stayed in during the pregnancy."

Later, when his mother could no longer care for him, Yader was placed in an orphanage. "We faced much adversity when we began pursuing him. We were literally told 'not a chance' and it was 'impossible' for us to adopt Yader." But after about eighteen months of 'no,' God again surprised the Crabtrees with a 'yes.' Jessie and her family split their time between their home-base in Missouri and the international mission field.

ALLISON CUNNINGHAM, //source, page 170

Allison is a teacher with a strong passion for knowing and understanding God's Word. "I love helping others apply spiritual and practical truth to their daily lives," says Allison. She has served in a variety of leadership roles in the local church, after receiving her pastoral license through Elim Fellowship.

The last two years have been a huge transition of expanding their family through adoption and moving from New Jersey to Tennessee. When asked to tell about how she likes to spend her time, Allison responded with, "Our family holds my heart and gets the biggest investment of my life. I enjoy coffee, cooking, bike riding, and getting to know people."

ALISHA FORREST //copy editor

Alisha Forrest is a freelance writer living in Nashville, Tennessee. She's married to her high school sweetheart and together they are in the middle of an adoption journey filled with more twists and turns than they ever could have anticipated. If she has learned one thing through all of this, it is simply to put faith first.

ANNE MARIE GOSNELL //purpose, page 112

Anne Marie says she and her husband weren't even married yet when they discussed that even if they did have biological children, they would still adopt. "When we went through years of infertility, and a miscarriage, I began researching different options. Five years and two biological miracles later, we seriously decided to begin the adoption process. It was October 2010, and my husband and I went through the Department of Social Service's training for adoption. We received the paperwork and we began the process. Our family began to pray for Baby #3."

Their adoption of a three-year-old girl was completed on July 17, 2014, but, as Anne Marie told us, "I had been praying for her since she was conceived. God knew she would need the protection of our prayers before she entered our home. God always has a purpose for times of waiting."

Anne Marie and her family live in South Carolina, where her husband is a Software Engineer and she is a classroom teacher turned into a home-school mom, and a Bible Teacher to children at her church.

Read more from Anne-Marie at **FUTUREFLYINGSAUCERS.COM**.

STACEY HARE //disappointment, page 66

Stacey, a California native, was married in 2003 to her husband Dave and a year later moved to Louisville, KY to study at The Southern Baptist Theological Seminary. There the couple decided to focus more specifically on the task of Bible translation in foreign missions. While in Kentucky, they started a pro-life ministry called "Speak for the Unborn" which seeks to mobilize the local church to "speak up" for the unborn.

While trying to get the ministry off the ground, Stacey and Dave adopted two children from Ethiopia. And after being exposed to the poverty in Africa, they determined to adopt two more children, one year later. "Once all the adoptions were finalized," Stacey confessed, "my husband and I looked around our dinner table and realized they had 4 children ages two and under. We both agree that parenting is far more difficult than anything they have experienced in ministry... but oh so rewarding."

RACHEL HARRISON //his presence, page 143

Rachel and her husband adopted two beautiful boys domestically. She is passionate about adoption and about supporting families who adopt in her community. She facilitates an adoption book club and provides training for families as they prepare for adoption. In addition to being a mom and adoption advocate, she has a counseling practice in Colorado, specializing in trauma.

Read more from Rachel at **WWW.DURANGOFAMILYTHERAPY.COM**.

TONJA IHLENFELDT //fear, page 48

Tonja works from home first as a wife and mother, and secondly as an artist. She has been happily married to my high school sweetheart for more than two dozen years. Together they have five biological children, two adopted children from Nicaragua, and now twin grandkids. "For over 25 years, I have been following after Jesus and," Tonja shares, "as a result our family, has been has been abundantly blessed."

See some of Tonja's artwork at **WWW.TONJAJ.COM**.

GLORYA JORDAN //spiritual warfare, page 105

Glorya Jordan is an open heart nurse by trade. She is currently the executive director of the Jordan household, managing three biological boys and one adopted little girl. She serves on the board for Care Net Resource Pregnancy

Center and speaks on foster and orphan care. She resides in Woodbridge, Virginia, with her husband, Darrell Jordan Jr., supporting him as a public servant for his church, community, and the state of Virginia.

WENDY LANKFORD //my shepherd, page 157

Wendy and her family live in Northeastern Maryland, where they serve the homeless population with The Open Table. In response to a request for her bio, Wendy told us this: "I'm nothing special. There is nothing remarkable about me. What is remarkable is that the same Voice that called the world into being calls my name. I'm in love with a pretend Scotsman, on the warpath for orphans and vulnerable people. I have two little hobbits who were born in my heart and can crust up a carpet like nobody's business. My latest baby has come from God in the form of a 21-year-old in need of a family, and a home, and a really tacky van to drive around for drivers ed. The more the merrier... or is it messier?" We decided we couldn't say it better ourselves ;-).

CARRIE LEISTER //faith, page 21

Carrie and her husband, Jamie, have been married for 18 years, and have two beautiful girls adopted from Nicaragua. Carrie works as a family practice physician assistant. She is also a worship leader in her church in Ohio. "Through our adoptions and serving in Nicaragua," Carrie tells us, "God has led Jamie and I to serve Him through Living Waters Fellowship for Missions, of which I am the president. One of my absolute favorite things is taking long walks on the beach hunting seashells with my girls, Sydney and Isabella."

MARY OSTYN //providence, page 136

Mary is the mother of four children by birth and six children through adoption, including four girls from Ethiopia and two boys from South Korea. Their first adopted child came home from South Korea in 1998. Their most recent adoption was in 2007, where they brought home two girls, ages 9 and 11, from Ethiopia.

Mary has written three books including: *Family Feasts for $75 a Week, A Sane Woman's Guide to Raising a Large Family*, and her most recent release, *Forever Mom: What to Expect When You're Adopting*. She speaks at adoption conferences and homeschooling conferences on a variety of mothering-related topics.

Read more from Mary at **WWW.OWLHAVEN.NET**.

LAURA PHENEGER //joy, page 60

Laura describes herself as a tennis playing, coffee sipping, missionary, and world-traveling mother of three, who, recently started blogging. Her husband is on staff with a sports ministry that allows them to travel throughout the U.S. and even abroad. Laura tells us she always said, "I am not an adoption person." But when she began experiencing some health issues after their second daughter was born, she and her husband felt God prompting us to consider adopting.

After the adoption was finalized, Laura launched a blog inspired by many years of travel and a desire to introduce children to other countries and cultures. You can join her at Mommy Maleta to explore the world "one suitcase at a time" and read about some of the ways God is caring for His children globally.

Read more from Laura at **WWW.MOMMYMALETA.COM**.

MELISSA SANDS //remembering, page 164
"Adoption has been on my heart for as long as I can remember," remembers Melissa. "I've spent many summers at camps as a counselor and was a special educator for over a decade in a large urban school district where I taught many foster children. I love kids especially the ones that many would consider a little rough around the edges."

Melissa and her husband, James, had two biological children before their adoption of a sweet little girl from China was finalized. The family makes their home in Maryland, where Melissa loves having moms over weekly for lunch and Bible studies. "We let the kids run amuck throughout the house while we share life and grow together in God's word," the Ohio native says with a smile. "I also love working with children and youth at our church. Spending time with my family and in God's word is important to me."

JESSICA SATTERFIELD //love, page 176
After loving on the orphans in Nicaragua over the summers of her college days, Jessica always knew her home would be filled with children who did not share her DNA. When she and her husband began to grow their family and were faced with the heartbreak of infertility, they both knew it was time to adopt.

They welcome their first child, Selah Grace, home through domestic adoption in 2013 and her half-sibling in April 2015. Jessica and her husband are on the leadership team of their church's orphan care ministry, Hope for Children, in Greenville, South Carolina. She encourages and mentors other adoptive moms online and through a Bible study held in her home.

Read more from Jessica at **GRACEWHILEWEWAIT.COM**.

ALLISON SCHUMM //loss, page 130
Adoptee Allison Schumm is an extremely passionate Titus 2 mom who strives to be a Proverbs 31 woman. She isn't perfect, in fact she would tell you the trauma and loss in her life makes her far from perfect, but she

strives to be the best wife to her husband Jonathan and mom to her 16 children. You got that right, 16! Being only 32, the math just doesn't work. She says her family tends to grow by twos and sixes. Jonathan and Allison have adopted two sibling groups of five (she was pregnant through both adoptions). Two more biological children are thrown into the mix and one of the sibling groups has since turned into a group of seven. Allison believes that sibling connections are one of the healthiest and stabilizing supports children can have through their journey.

Allison home schools her small army, and is passionate about helping her children heal and become the best individuals they can be. In her "free time" Allison loves to write and provide adoption consultation and training through Kansas's statewide adoption ministry Project Belong.

MICHELLE SIMPSON //humility, page 92
After surrendering her heart to Christ in college, Cincinnati-native Michelle served Him first as an overseas missionary, and then working with inner-city youth, which led to a Master's degree in counseling.

"However, it was in the roles of wife and mother that God really began to refine the deepest, most hidden parts of my heart as He asked me to lay down my life for my family," shares Michelle. "Just ten days shy of our one-year anniversary, my husband Ricky and I welcomed our imaginative son Isaac into the world and then his beautiful sister Emma followed 18 months later. Shortly before Emma was born, God clearly placed the call to adopt on my life and less than 3 years later, our whole family stood in China with our precious little boy Josiah!"

The family resides in Frederick, Maryland, where Ricky is the Associate Pastor at their church.

MELISSA STANEK //waiting, page 118
"About eight years into marriage," Melissa recalls, "God decided to speak to our family about adoption. It happened one night at a Steven Curtis Chapman concert. At one point in the evening, Steven spoke specifically about adoption. My husband and I were so moved, that we were both crying. That night, we decided to adopt."

After several years and much prayer, God directed them to adopt from the country of Poland. It took many more years—and a ton of waiting—but this Ohio family is now, finally, a party of five. Their oldest two are teenagers, and Anya became a US citizen, at two-and-a-half, on Sept 11, 2013.

JULIE SWAIN //beholding Christ, page 40 //anger, page 98
Julie married her best friend and earthly love of her life, Ben, in the winter of 2008. They then began the journey of growing as a family, discovering one day before their first anniversary that they were expecting their first

son. When their son was about three months old, the couple felt the desire to adopt in such a way that they knew God was calling them someday to open their home to a child who didn't have one.

After welcoming another son, they traveled to China, and held their daughter, Selah Grace, for the first time before finally bringing her home a few weeks later. "It has been a wild ride for sure!" tells Julie. "Everyday we desire to walk in the measure of grace God has given us, and we long to cling to him as he has so tightly clung to us. Adoption has been the vehicle God used to set our eyes on Christ in such a different way, beholding him for all he's done in the midst of what we are helpless to do on our own."

LISA WILLIAMS //his faithfulness, page 150
Lisa grew up in Alaska and currently lives in Alabama. She worked for an adoption agency for five years, where she provided education and support for adoptive families. Adoption became a lot more personal when she and her husband struggled with infertility for years and experienced two miscarriages. One of those included a loss of a daughter at 14 weeks..

God first placed adoption on Lisa heart years ago when she read, *Adopted for Life; The Priority of Adoption for Christian Families and Churches* by Russell D. Moore. The couple prayerfully decided to adopt from Russia, which requires three separate trips. Two days after returning from their second trip, Lisa suffered a brain stem stroke, and was not able to go on the final trip because she was still in the hospital. The effects of the stroke caused major difficulties with attachment and bonding. Almost two years later, Lisa is still in a wheelchair and has a lot of other challenges. Through it all, the Lord has been faithful.

Read more from Lisa at **WHILEWAITINGIWILLWORSHIP.BLOGSPOT.COM**.

TAMMY WONDRA //hope, page 72
Tammy and her husband have been married for 13 years and live in Wisconsin. The couple struggled with infertility for eight years. "God called us to adopt after a miscarriage in April 2011 and our daughter was born in December 2011," recalls Tammy. "Our story is full of miracles and God truly shows His hand in the part of bringing our daughter into our lives."

Tammy works at home as a medical transcriptionist. Her husband, Mark, is disabled due to some medical issues, but Tammy says, "God continues to show us His wonderful blessings and provides us with so much more than we deserve and we live each day striving to live for Him."

Read more from Tammy at **WWW.TWONDRA.BLOGSPOT.COM**.

scripture

Genesis 3:7-8	Day 1 //loss, 131
Genesis 3:21	Day 1 //loss, 131
Genesis 12:1	Day 5 //waiting, 123
Genesis 15:4	Day 1 //waiting, 119
Genesis 16:1-16	Day 1 //love, 179
Genesis 37, 39-41	Day 1 //his faithfulness, 152
Genesis 45:7	Day 5 //providence, 142
Exodus 2:1-10	Day 1 //adoption, 9
Exodus 14:10-31	providence, 136
Exodus 14:15-31	Day 1 //remembering, 165
Exodus 16	Day 1 //remembering, 165
Exodus 17	Day 1 //remembering, 165
Deuteronomy 31:6	Day 2 //loss, 132
Deuteronomy 34:4	Day 1 //remembering, 165
Joshua 1:7-9	Day 5 //spiritual warfare, 111
Joshua 4	Day 4 //waiting, 122
Joshua 4:2-9	Day 5 //remembering, 169
1 Samuel 1:1-16	barrenness, 27
I Kings 19: 1-18	his presence, 143
Esther 2:5-7	Day 2 //adoption, 11
Esther 4:13-14	Day 2 //adoption, 11
Ezekial 21:4	Day 3 //hope, 75
Ezekiel 34: 11-16	my shepherd, 157
Psalm 4:8	Day 3 //providence, 140
Psalm 16:1	Day 5 //disappointment, 71
Psalm 16:11	Day 3 //joy, 63
Psalm 27:6	Day 4 //joy, 64
Psalm 37:4	faith, 21
Psalm 40:1-3	Day 2 //waiting, 120
Psalm 46:10	Day 2 //self-care, 17
Psalm 47:1-3	Day 4 //joy, 64
Psalm 71:23	Day 4 //joy, 64
Psalm 86:17	Day 4 //remembering, 168
Psalm 88: 1-18	Day 1 //depression, 80
Psalm 92:4-5	Day 5 //joy, 65
Psalm 113:9	faith, 21
	DAY 5 //barrenness, 33
Psalm 119:105	Day 2 //providence, 139
Psalm 121:1-2	Day 3 //waiting, 121
Psalm 138:3	Day 2 //peace, 172
Psalm 138:8	Day 2 //peace, 172
	Day 3 //barrenness, 31
Psalm 139:1-5	Day 1 //self-care, 16
Psalm 139:1-18	anger, 98
Psalm 139:16	Day 1 //disappointment, 67
Psalm 145	failure, 85
Proverbs 21:1	Day 3 //worry, 37
Ecc. 4:9-12	Day 4 //depression, 83
Isaiah 25:8-9	Day 5 //disappointment, 71
Isaiah 41:10	Day 2 //peace, 172
	Day 1 //fear, 49
Isaiah 43:4	Day 1 //self-care, 16
Isaiah 43:18-19	Day 1 //barrenness, 29
Isaiah 53	Day 4 //loss, 134
Isaiah 53:4-6	Day 5 //love, 183
Isaiah 55:8	Day 3 //remembering, 167
Isaiah 55:9	Day 1 //waiting, 119
Isaiah 58:11	Day 2 //peace, 172
Jeremiah 29:11	Day 4 //barrenness, 32
	Day 5 //providence, 142
	Day 2 //remembering, 166
Jeremiah 32:27	Day 2 //peace, 172
Hosea 2:14-23	Day 2 //love, 180
Matthew 1:18-25	Day 3 //adoption, 12
Matthew 4:23-25	Day 5 //self-care, 20
Matthew 7:1-6	Day 3 //self-care, 18
Matthew 10:29-31	Day 3 //barrenness, 31
Mark 11:24	Day 4 //disappointment, 70
Mark 15:34	Day 1 //loss, 131
Luke 2:11-12	Day 3 //remembering, 167
Luke 2:19	Day 1 //remembering, 165
Luke 6:32-33, 35-36	Day 3 //disappointment, 69
Luke 11:9-13	trust, 54
Luke 15:7	Day 3 //loss, 133
Luke 22:41-43	Day 2 //depression, 81
	Day 3 //depression, 82
Luke 22:42-44	Day 5 //loss, 135
Luke 23:4	Day 4 //loss, 134
Luke 23:34	Day 4 //loss, 134
John 8:1-11	Day 4 //love, 182
John 10:10	Day 3 //his faithfulness, 154
John 14:13-14	Day 4 //trust, 58
John 14:26	Day 4 //depression, 83
John 14:27	Day 3 //peace, 173
John 15:7	Day 1 //trust, 55
John 16:24	Day 5 //trust, 59
	Day 4 //disappointment, 70

John 16:33	*Day 3 //hope, 75*	2 Timothy 1:7	*Day 5 //peace, 175*
	Day 5 //depression, 84		
John 20:24-29	*Day 3 //love, 181*	Hebrews 4:12	*Day 4 //peace, 174*
		Hebrews 10:35-36	*Day 2 //waiting, 120*
Romans 2:6-8	*Day 3 //disappointment, 69*	Hebrews 11:1	*faith, 21*
Romans 5:1-5	*endurance, 124*	Hebrews 12:1-2, 7-11	*purpose, 112*
Romans 5:2-5	*hope, 72*		
Romans 8:28	*Day 3 //waiting, 121*	James 1:2-3	*Day 2 //joy, 62*
	Day 4 //his faithfulness, 155		*Day 3 //endurance, 127*
	Day 5 //peace, 175	James 1:12	*Day 4 //endurance, 128*
Romans 8:32	*Day 1 //loss, 131*		*Day 5 //loss, 135*
Romans 12:2	*Day 4 //spiritual warfare, 110*	James 1:13-15	*Day 4 //spiritual warfare, 110*
Romans 12:12	*Day 2 //endurance, 126*	James 1:22	*Day 5 //peace, 175*
		James 1:27	*Day 5 //adoption, 14*
1 Cor. 6:19-20	*Day 5 //self-care, 20*		*DAY 5 //barrenness, 33*
1 Cor. 7:29-31	*Day 5 //disappointment, 71*		*Day 4 //waiting, 122*
1 Cor. 9:24	*Day 5 //endurance, 129*		
2 Cor. 4:6-18	*beholding Christ, 40*	1 Peter 5:8-9	*Day 1 //spiritual warfare, 107*
2 Cor. 4:16-18	*hope, 72*		
2 Cor. 4:17	*Day 2 //spiritual warfare, 108*	1 John 2:14b-17	*Day 3 //spiritual warfare, 109*
2 Cor. 9:8	*Day 2 //disappointment, 68*	1 John 4:4	*Day 5 //depression, 84*
2 Cor. 10:3-5	*Day 5 //peace, 175*	1 John 4:18	*Day 2 //fear, 50*
2 Cor. 12:7-9a	*Day 2 //disappointment, 68*		
2 Cor. 12:9	*Day 5 //depression, 84*	Revelation 2:10b	*Day 1 //joy, 61*
	Day 1 //failure, 87		
	Day 5 //peace, 175		
Galatians 3:26	*Day 4 //adoption, 13*		
Galatians 4:4-7	*Day 4 //adoption, 13*		
	Day 2 //loss, 132		
Galatians 5:22	*Day 3 //humility, 95*		
Ephesians 1:5	*Day 1 //worry, 35*		
Ephesians 2:4-7	*Day 1 //loss, 131*		
Ephesians 2:10	*Day 3 //barrenness, 31*		
Ephesians 3:20-21	*Day 5 //trust, 59*		
	Day 5 //remembering, 169		
Ephesians 6:12	*Day 3 //his faithfulness, 154*		
Ephesians 6:10-18	*spiritual warfare, 105*		
Ephesians 6:14-17	*Day 3 //his faithfulness, 154*		
Philippians 1:3-11	*Day 4 //self-care, 19*		
Philippians 1:6	*Day 3 //humility, 95*		
Philippians 2:1-11	*humility, 92*		
Philippians 4:4, 5b	*Day 1 //joy, 61*		
Philippians 4:4-9	*worry, 34*		
	fear, 48		
	peace, 170		
Philippians 4:8	*adoption, 8*		
Colossians 1:11	*Day 5 //endurance, 129*		
1 Thes. 5:18	*Day 4 //waiting, 122*		

in all things give thanks...

(1 Thessalonians 5:18a)

This book is the culmination of years of grace and mercy in the lives of so many families. It is the result of a chorus of yeses, even amidst waves of doubt and fear. I am so grateful for all moms who say yes to adoption, yes to daily self-sacrifice, and yes to sharing their stories.

The women who have contributed to this book are amazing testaments to God's power and redemption. I am so humbled and honored to have written alongside of them, so thankful to call them friends. And I am so grateful to everyone who has helped make this dream a reality.

I pray for all who are following in God's very own footsteps, walking this path of adoption. This road isn't easy. I've watched so many attempt to walk it alone, and know the devastation that can bring. I pray he uses this book to strengthen and encourage you, drawing you closer to him in the process. Because, dear friend, *you are worth it*. Through Christ, *you are capable*. With Christ, *you are enough*.

In him,

Wendy

P.S. We at FIT (Families in Transition) Global want to grow the concept of adoption care, where we walk alongside adopting families no matter where they are in the process. All proceeds from this book benefit adopting families through this mission. Learn more about our first project at **WWW.FITNICARAGUA.ORG**, or by contacting me at my personal blog, **WWW.STILLNOTTHEREYET.COM**.

P.P.S. If you've loved reading this book as much as we've loved building it, could you help spread the word? Post a review on Amazon, share the link on Facebook, or give a copy to another adopting mom. And praise God for connecting us together in this manner.

Made in the USA
San Bernardino, CA
10 November 2015